Honor Among First-Gen Arab Women

Ayser Al Bara' Abboud

Abstract

Since the terrorist attacks of 9/11, there has been a significant amount of research on the Middle East and Islam. These studies inform the academic community regarding the culture and religion of the region and its people. An area of research regarding the culture and people of the Middle East that has not been represented in the literature is the experience of honor. Honor has been researched from a sociological and anthropological perspective, and honor killings have been present in the media. However, there was a need for the experience of honor, specifically among first generation Levantine Arab American women, to be explored in a qualitative study. The methodology used for this study was Moustakas' heuristic research design, which allowed the primary researcher to illuminate the experience of honor among first generation Levantine Arab American women. The study found that honor was a complex experience for the participants. The multifaceted experience was familial and societal, public and private, and individual and collective. The experience of honor among first generation Levantine Arab American women was found to be one that started in early childhood and continued into adulthood, never really ending for the participant. The participants describe their lives as a struggle between the wants of the individual and the wants of the family and community. The implications of the study are discussed further in Chapter 5.

Table of Contents

CHAPTER 1. INTRODUCTION

Background of the Problem (Introduction)

Honor killings have been occurring for centuries in cultures across the globe

(Jafri, 2008). There is a higher concentration of honor killings in the Middle East;

however, there have been increased rates of immigration from Muslim and Arab

countries (D'Agostino, 2002; Kayyali, 2005). With the increased rates of immigration,

there has also been a significant increase in the rates of honor killing in the United States,

specifically between 1989 and 2009 (Chesler, 2010). These honor killings are occurring

in Texas, where Amina and Sarah Said were shot dead by their father for having

boyfriends (Spencer, 2008). It has happened in Ohio, where Lubaina Ahmed and her 2-

year-old daughter were found with their throats slit by her husband for filing for divorce

(Ackerman & Block, 1999). Again, it occurred in Georgia, where Sandeela Kanwal was

strangled to death by her father for refusing an arranged marriage (Tarabay, 2009), and in

New York, when a TV executive beheaded his estranged wife when she filed for divorce

(Shahram, 2009). Once again in Arizona, Aasiya Hassan was also beheaded by her

husband for filing for divorce (Robbins, 2009). In New Jersey, Nashish Noorani was shot

dead by her husband for allegedly being unfaithful (Stelloh & Barron, 2011). These

young women who were attacked and murdered in the name of honor are immigrants and

children of immigrants, first and second generation. Their lives were affected by the

concept of honor held by Muslim and Arab communities. The concept of honor is multifaceted and has cultural, social, religious, and moral facets, which determine how it is understood and expressed. To understand the concept of honor killings, there needs to be an understanding of honor, as it is experienced by these women.

This research study began as a way to understand the lived experience of honor of these women to further understand the phenomenon of honor killings, which is happening more frequently in the Western world and the United States. Honor killing is a violent crime against a woman that is usually premeditated and carried out by male members of the female's family (Shaikh, Shaikh, Kamal, & Masood, 2010). Honor killings occur when a woman has been accused of committing an act that is deemed dishonorable, such as premarital sex, infidelity, or inappropriate interactions with the opposite sex (Nasrullah, Haqqi, & Cummings, 2009). The women, who have committed these offenses or other in the same vein, are seen as having damaged the family's honor. Those who commit the honor killing do so in order to remove the shame of the dishonorable act committed by the female. These gender-based killings are occurring more frequently across the globe and are contributing to the mortality rates of women (Nasrullah et al., 2009). While honor killings are not solely a Muslim issue, it is quickly becoming associated with Islam as these killings occur in Muslim communities but also occur in European societies as well (Doğan, 2011).

This study was developed to discover and understand the lived experience of honor among Levantine Arab American women ages 25-35 using Moustakas' (1990) method of heuristic research. The research question is "What is the lived experience of honor among first generation Levantine Arab American women?" By utilizing the heuristic process, the researcher was able to create a knowledge base about the lived experience of honor for Levantine Arab American women, ages 25-35. There is a significant amount of research in the fields of Islam, women and Islam, Islam in America, immigration and acculturation, honor, and honor killings (Abdo, 2006; Ahmed, 1992; Amer & Hovey, 2007; Abu-Odeh, 2010; Bailey, 2009; Barlas, 2002; Beck & Keddie, 1980; Boosahda. 2003; Chesler, 2010; D'Agostino, 2002; Esposito, 2002a; Faragallah, Schumm, & Webb, 1997; Faqir, 2001; Gilmore, 1987; Haddad, 1991, 2011; Hassan, 2000; Husseini, 2009; Madek, 2005; Peristiany & Pitt-Rivers, 1992; Peristiany, 1965; Stewart, 1994; Wadud, 1999; Zentella, 2010).

However, there had been virtually no research on the lived experience of honor among Levantine Arab American women. Studying the lived experience of honor among Arab American women provided an opportunity to begin to understand the impact of honor in the Levantine Arab American woman's life.

Statement of the Problem

There has been a great deal of research on the topic of honor in the literature; with significant findings related to the effects it has on mental health. The effects are generally organized into three areas: the self, the family, and the community (Dwairy, 1997; Hodge & Nadir, 2008; Hopkins, 2001; Krause, 1995; Nassar-McMillan & Hakim-Larson, 2003; Sayed, 2003; Smith, 2011; Timimi, 1995). The majority of the current research on honor has been qualitative mental health studies that focused on teaching psychologists about how to become more culturally competent in regards to Arab individual, the family and the community (Dwairy, 1997; Sayed, 2003; Timimi, 1995). These studies focused on the cultural competence of the psychologist and how to understand the Arab patient to gain the trust of the patient through an understanding of the patient's culture. Developing a better understanding of the lived experience of honor among Levantine first generation Arab American women has contributed to closing the gap in the literature between the study of honor and the application of cultural competence of psychologists in the Arab American community.

The focus of this study was to explore and discover the lived experience of honor among Levantine first generation Arab American women. It was the intent of this study to contribute knowledge to the field of psychology, particularly related to cultural competence. The understanding gained in this study about the lived experience of honor among Levantine first generation Arab American women will capture the complexity of the life of the Levantine Arab American women. There is a careful balance between the wants and needs of the self versus the wants and needs of the family. The information brought forth from this study provided further insight into the concept of honor and how it is experienced. Through the research, the researcher aimed to better understand the lived experience of honor among Levantine Arab American women. The researcher also looked to develop a deeper understanding of the interconnectedness of culture, gender, and religion in the Levantine community.

Purpose of the Study

The purpose of this research study was to gain a deeper understanding of the concept of honor and the lived experience of honor. In addition, this study was meant to add to the psychological literature base related to honor and fill the gap in qualitative literature investigating honor, as there are no qualitative studies to be found on the subject. As was previously discussed, this research study began with an interest in honor killings and their occurrence in the Western world. The study evolved into a study focused on understanding honor itself. Specifically, to learn about what it is like to experience honor as a Levantine first generation Arab American woman, between the ages of 25-35 using Moustakas' (1990) method of heuristic research. The heuristic approach and its ability to develop a meaningful understanding of an experience are summed up well by Moustakas (1990) when he states:

> The power of heuristics is in its recognition of the significance of self-searching and the value of personal knowledge as essential requirements for the understanding of common human experience. There is no substitute for direct, comprehensive, accurate first person accounts of experience, for the importance of self-inquiry and self-dialogue in discovering the nature and meaning of one's own experience and that of others. (p. 90)

Having lived a life where honor is at the forefront of her consciousness, this researcher has encountered the struggle and impact of honor in her daily life. She chose to research the lived experience of honor to better understand the essence of the lived experience and to better understand the experience as it is experienced by others. The heuristic model aligned well with this researcher's qualitative paradigm related to research, and as a Levantine first generation Arab American woman she met the requirements of Moustakas' (1990) scientific model. Finally, studying the lived experience of honor among Levantine Arab American women added to the literature in the field of honor by discovering the role and impact of honor in the everyday lives of the women interviewed.

Significance of the Study

The focus of this study was to explore the lived experience of honor among women who identified themselves as Levantine first generation Arab American. These women were of interest due to their exposure to Islam and Arab culture. Given the emerging importance of honor and Islam in the United States, exploring the Arab American experience of honor was significant to the field of general psychology (Abdo, 2006; Abu-Odeh, 2010; Bailey, 2009; Boosahda. 2003; Chesler, 2010; Faqir, 2001; Gilmore, 1987; Haddad, 1991, 2011; Hassan, 2000; Husseini, 2009; Madek, 2005; Peristiany & Pitt-Rivers, 1992; Peristiany, 1965; Stewart, 1994).

As a result of their culture and upbringing, what was the experience of honor of the Levantine first generation Arab American woman? The information brought forth from this study has brought researchers one step closer towards an understanding about the experience of honor. America is the melting pot of culture and custom. As we move towards a more integrated society, it was wise to identify components of a community that is not only growing but has an effect on its people.

Research Design

The research model used was Moustakas' (1990) heuristic approach. The researcher is a part of the community being studied and the data collected from her input as well as the co-researchers will allow a vivid picture to be illustrated of the lived experience of honor in first generation Levantine Arab American women. According to Moustakas (1990), heuristic inquiry is "a process of internal search through which one discovers the nature and meaning of experience" (p. 9). This study aims to understand the nature and meaning of the lived experience of honor in first generation Levantine Arab American women. A defining aspect of heuristic inquiry is that the researcher's experience is also included in the data. In addition, a requirement of heuristic inquiry is that the researcher must have a vested and intense interest in the topic to be studied.

6

Phases of Heuristic Research and Data Analysis

There are six phases of heuristic research: initial engagement, immersion, incubation, illumination, explication, and creative synthesis. Moustakas (1990) described initial engagement as "the investigator reaching inward for tacit awareness and knowledge, permits intuition to run freely, and elucidates the context from which the questions take form and significance" (p. 27). It is during this phase the researcher is allowing the research question to take shape. What is the problem? What is the question we want answered? In the second phase of heuristic research, immersion, the researcher delves into the study. The researcher submerges their mind into the data, the participants, and the research question. Moustakas' (1990) third phase of heuristic inquiry is incubation. Incubation enables the researcher to take a moment and to reflect on the process of research and just marinate in the data collected. Here, the researcher is focusing on the emerging discussion and not so much on the question being asked. The fourth phase is illumination, the moment where the researcher is about to see the emergent themes within the data, the patterns within the data. The fourth phase is where the researcher is able to start to piece together the parts of the experience of the individual. Once the themes from the data collected are revealed, the fifth phase of heuristic inquiry takes place. The fifth phase of heuristic inquiry is explication, the point in the study where the pieces of information are examined individually before they are examined as a whole. It is here in this phase, the researcher is now able to piece together the experience of the individual and create a whole piece of lived experience. In the final and sixth phase of heuristic inquiry, creative synthesis, the researcher finally puts the pieces of data together to create a whole picture of the findings. The data has been analyzed, the themes and patterns have emerged, and an illustrative picture of the experience is painted. At this point, the researcher is already quite familiar with the data and participants, and is now able to discuss the findings of the study in a narrative form. Heuristic inquiry delves into the deepest and most complex human experiences. Both the participants and the researcher felt these experiences. The intense shared experience differentiates heuristic research from other methodologies, such as grounded theory, phenomenological, etc. The question asked in heuristic research is always a question of how does one experience a phenomenon. The researcher becomes a participant and the participants become co-researchers. Both the participants and researcher learn and grow during this study. Understanding and illustrating a lived experience is completely coordinated using heuristic inquiry.

Sampling

Moustakas (1990) discussed heuristic scientist as seeking "to discover the nature and meaning of the phenomenon itself and to illuminate it from the direct first-person accounts of individuals who have directly encountered the phenomenon in experience" (p. 38). Due to the nature of the individuals required for a heuristic study, the researcher chose to use intensity sampling to recruit participants. A qualitative heuristic research study, using intensity sampling, was chosen because the phenomenon to be studied is the lived experience of honor among Levantine first generation Arab American Women. In using intensity sampling, the sample consists of "information-rich cases that manifest the phenomenon of interest intensely" (Patton, 1990, p. 171). The focus in this type of sampling is the intensity of the experience not the frequency of occurrence, this type of sampling compliments heuristic study well.

Data Collection Methods

As previously mentioned, the researcher printed and posted flyers for the recruitment of participants around the Muslim Community Center. The flyer contained the researcher's contact information. As each participant responded, the researcher screened the participant to ensure eligibility. A meeting time with the participant was arranged, at their convenience. The location of the meeting was held in a private room in a local library. The researcher reserved a private room to conduct the interviews. The data collection required a study that would shed light on and expand on the lived experience of honor, rather than measuring it and its frequency of appearance.

The room contained the researcher's laptop for recording, the researcher's notebook for field notes, and water for the participant. The researcher waited for the participant at the door of the room, after giving detailed directions as how to find them. Once the participant made their way to the room, the researcher greeted them. In this greeting, the researcher informed the participant of their first name, a brief background describing the researcher's Middle Eastern origin, and gave the participant a moment to ask any questions the participant might have. At this meeting, the researcher described the nature of the study and provided a consent form to the participant. The participant was given time to review the consent form and time to ask any questions regarding the consent form.

Once the participants were screened to fit the study's criteria, the researcher organized interview times. The consent forms were read and signed, and the recorded informal, conversational interviews began. Regarding data collection, the researcher utilized opened ended questions during a conversational interview. The participants were asked to keep a journal with their written answers to the guiding research questions, as

they may differ from (or they may add to) what is brought up during the interviews. A

prepaid, addressed envelope was provided with the journal so that the participant may

mail it back to the researcher with minimal imposition. The researcher requested that the

journals are sent back within four weeks of the interview. The participant may choose not

to participate in the journaling. At the end of each interview, the researcher wrote down

any ideas, questions, or thoughts that came to her. Those notes were transcribed into the

researcher's computer at the end of each interview along with the recorded sessions with

each participant. The interviews were recorded with the permission of the participants.

The researcher recorded field notes immediately after each interview; those notes were

transcribed into the researcher's computer at the end of each interview along with the

recorded sessions with each participant. The journal with the researcher's and

participants' data is kept in a password protected file on the researcher's computer which

is also password protected, to ensure the participant's privacy. As part of the heuristic

process, the researcher collected her own data by answering the research question and the

interview questions in a journal.

After all the interviews had been conducted, the researcher sent the recordings to

a transcribing service. The transcriber signed a confidentiality agreement before

accessing the data for transcription. Once all the data had been documented, the

researcher began the analysis of the recorded (audio and journals) and transcribed data.

Data Analysis Methods

Moustakas (1990) provided an eight-step outline of procedures of the analysis of

the data collected during a heuristic study. The researcher utilized the eight-step process in the analyzing of the data collected during this study. The first step in the course of analyzing data is the collecting of the data. All the researcher's notes, journals, and transcribed interviews are to be collected at this stage. The second stage called for the researcher to immerse herself in the data until the researcher fully understands the experience as it is presented. In the third stage, the researcher left the data for a period. In this time, the researcher has gained a fresh perspective on the material collected. Once the researcher returned to the material, the researcher was able to identify the emergent themes and patterns in the data. In the fourth stage of data analysis, the researcher returns to the data and answered the questions of "does the individual depiction of the experience fit the data from which it was developed? Does it contain the qualities and themes essential to the experience?" (Moustakas, 1990, p. 51). Once the researcher answered these questions for the first participant, she moved on to subsequent participants, which fulfills the fifth step of analysis.

The sixth step called for the researcher to gather the experiences of all the participants. Once gathered, the researcher studied the data until all emergent themes and patterns were uncovered. It was at this portion of the analysis the researcher can develop a composite depiction of the experience as a whole. In the seventh step of data analysis, Moustakas (1990) calls for another return to the raw data. The researcher chose three participants that best depict the experience being studied. The researcher developed a picture of the experience being studied using direct quotes, images, and the participant's narratives. The eighth and final step of data analysis as outlined by Moustakas (1990) is the development of creative synthesis. Utilizing the data, the processes of data collection and her own experience, the researcher created a clear and illustrative depiction of the experience using the themes and patterns discovered.

Data Presentation Methods

The findings of the study are presented in *Chapter 4: Data Collection and Analysis*. The findings are presented in a manner that is consistent with the heuristic methodology. Following the description of each participant and the description of the sample as a whole, the key themes of each participant's experience are presented sequentially, followed by illustrative quotes regarding the themes that illuminate the experience. The emergent themes were analyzed and presented to each participant. These quotes allow for an understanding of the experience from the perspective of the participant. Following the presentation of the emergent themes in the data, the researcher generated emergent patterns in the data. Illustrative quotes regarding the patterns were utilized to present a clear understanding of each pattern presented. The emergent patterns were analyzed and presented to each participant.

Following the presentation of the emergent themes and patterns for each participant, the researcher presented a composite collective. In this composite, the researcher used the participant's narrative, the language, and the verbatim words captured in interviews. With this composite, the researcher creates a vivid and illustrative picture of the whole lived experience. In addition, the researcher presented a few cases that best exemplified the lived experience of honor as a whole. The researcher chose three participants and spotlighted each participant's experience, interview, and journal. The researcher also used direct quotes from the participant's interviews and journals to illustrate further the experience.

Research Questions and Hypotheses

The central research question for this heuristic study was "What is the lived experience of honor among Levantine first generation Arab American women between the ages of 25 and 35?" In regards to qualitative studies and hypothesis, there are no hypotheses created before the study is implemented. In regards to heuristics, the focus is "on the recreation of the lived experience; full and complete depictions of the experience from the frame of reference of the experiencing person" (Moustakas, 1990, p. 39). There is no hypothesis for the researcher to prove, just an experience to illuminate. The importance of the research question is explained by Moustakas (1990) as "the awakening of such a question comes through an inward clearing, and an intentional readiness and determination to discover a fundamental truth regarding the meaning and essence of one's own experience and that of others" (p. 40). The experience and the question are the focal point throughout the study, not the proving or disproving of a hypothesis.

Assumptions and Limitations

Theoretical and Topical Assumptions

There are a number of theoretical and topical assumptions in this study. It is assumed that the Levant was a sufficient geographical area to fit into the study of the lived experience of honor. It is assumed that honor is a social, cultural, religious, familial, geographical, and political practice (Abu-Odeh, 2010; Doğan, 2011; Eisner & Ghuneim, 2013; Faqir, 2001; Gilmore, 1987; Husseini, 2009; Leung & Cohen, 2011; Madek, 2005; Peristiany, 1965, Stewart, 1994). Stewart (1994) discussed honor as having two

13

components, "One is 'objectified honor', which is a person's good reputation, the other 'subjectified honor', is a person's sense of their self-worth" (p. 34).

Methodological Assumptions

A number of methodological assumptions were important to the heuristic approach of this study. The first assumption was that qualitative research should honor the participants' voice and experiences as an intricate part of the research process (Moustakas, 1990). The researcher allowed the full illustration of the experience, based on the experience of the participant, to be expressed. In regards to ontological assumptions and heuristic research, the experience is composed of parts. "The focus in a heuristic quest is on a recreation of the lived experience; full and complete depictions of the experience from the frame of reference of the experiencing person" (Moustakas, 1990, p. 39). After the parts are analyzed and reviewed by the researcher, they express a whole picture of the experience as constructed by the participants.

The epistemological assumption was that through the understanding of the individual's lived experience, the researcher would be able to decrease the distance between herself and the participant. In Moustakas' (1990) heuristic research, the researcher is "receiving the other as a partner, accepting and affirming the other person" (p. 47). In doing so, they are validating the experience, sharing the experience, and closing the distance between the researcher and participant. This assumption also ties into a specific heuristic assumption of self-reflexivity. This concept is understood as two individuals with the same lived experience, one researcher, and one participant, can explore and understand the others' experiences without influencing the outcome in a significant way, based on his/her own bias. It is believed that both the ontological and epistemological assumptions yielded data from the participants that would be

scientifically valid.

Topical Assumptions

It is assumed that the chosen age range was appropriate in regards to the

phenomenon being studied. It was assumed the participants shared the interest in honor.

Finally, it was assumed that the heuristic approach was the best approach to answering

the research question rather than an alternate qualitative design. In addition, this research

study assumed that the participants were honest during their interviews. It is assumed that

the Levantine first generation Arab American woman was a sufficient population to

answer the research question. It is assumed that the participants will have genuine honor

experience. It is assumed that the experience of honor can be researched and expressed

utilizing the heuristic methodology.

Limitations

Some areas of weakness were a part of this study's qualitative design that could

not be helped due to the researcher's choice on heuristics as a methodology. Generally, in

heuristic research the sample size is smaller than other methodologies (Moustakas, 1990),

as it allows for a more in-depth look at the phenomenon. The smaller sample size reduced

generalizability but allowed for the exploration of an unusual phenomenon, the

experience of honor. However, since the co-researchers were from the states of New

York, New Jersey, Connecticut, Massachusetts, California, Nevada, Wyoming, and

Florida, and there was a consistency of experience, credibility was increased. In addition,

the participants were from various parts of the Levant in the Middle East. Therefore,

there are specific depictions of all of the Middle East as a whole. The researcher was deeply involved in this study. This is a required component of heuristic research and during the process, the researcher practiced restraint in regards to biases that could have affected the study. Finally, the last limitation in this study was that although the researcher did have qualitative data analysis experience, the researcher did not specifically have experience in heuristic inquiry.

Definition of Terms

Arab American. Arab Americans are individuals of Arab decent and born in the United States. The parents of these individuals may or may not be naturalized citizens of the United States.

First Generation. First generation is women in the study whose parents are not American born citizens, who did not live in the United States from birth to 25 (born and raised in the Levant), and who have immigrated to the United States and had children. Those female children are the first generation Arab American women.

Honor. There are many definitions of what constitutes honor. However, for this study the definition discussed by Frank Henderson Stewart is utilized. Anthropologist Frank Henderson Stewart (1994) discussed Honor as having two components, "One is 'objectified honor,' which is a person's good reputation, the other 'subjectified honor,' is a person's sense of their self-worth" (p. 34).

Levantine. Being of Middle Eastern descent from the following countries Lebanon, Syria, Jordan, Egypt, Palestinian territories, and Israel.

Lived Experience. "A lived experience does not confront me as something perceived or represented; it is not given to me, but the reality of lived experience is there-for-me because I have a reflexive awareness of it, because I possess it immediately as belonging to me in some sense, and only in thought does it become objective" (Van

Manen, 1990 p. 35).

Women. The women who will participate in this study are first generation,

Levantine, Arab Americans who are between the ages of 25-35.

Expected Findings

On the heuristic research method, it is understood that this study was a process of

discovery and exploration. As such, there was no assumption of expected findings.

Rather, the researcher approached the research question with an open mind as to allow

the lived experience of others to arise (Moustakas, 1990). Integrity and the researcher's

own self-awareness were practiced the entirety of the study to reduce the researcher's

bias. The researcher expected that the heuristic process would lead to the understanding

of the lived experience of honor.

Role of the Researcher

It can be difficult for a researcher, who has experience with the phenomenon

being studied, not to bring their own bias into the study, which could taint the data being

collected. To help reduce this, the researcher has identified any possible biases and has

laid out the methods to eliminate them. The researcher is a 32-year-old first generation,

Levantine, Arab American woman. Honor has played, and still plays, a significant role in

the researcher's life. It has affected her decisions regarding schooling, social activities,

clothing, dating, her professional choices, and her personal choices. The researcher

assumed that all first generation, Levantine, Arab American women live with the mindset

that the individual choices come secondary to the choices of the family, to the honor of

17

the family. The researcher has lived with the concept of honor affecting her daily life. It was assumed by the researcher that honor has affected the day-to-day lives of the participants and has affected their lived experience as a whole. There was a preconceived notion on the part of the researcher that all first generation, Levantine, Arab American women have had similar experiences regarding the role of honor and the impact on their lives. The researcher assumed the responses and experiences would be similar to hers, in that all the participants would have had a negative experience of honor in their lives. The researcher understood that this might not have been the experience of honor for all the participants in the study. The researcher's experience was used to inform the research question, provide sensitivity and understanding during the interview process, and give the study an additional resource in regards to data.

The researcher's experience with the phenomenon raised concerns regarding the outcome being influenced. Previous knowledge and the researcher's bias were set aside to attain a fresh perspective on the participant's words, ideas, and experiences. To reduce the influence of biases, the researcher began initial data collection with her own personal knowledge of the experience. In collecting her own data first, the researcher was then able to suspend or close off her own experiences and beliefs regarding honor and the lived experience. In collecting her data first, through recorded responses and journaling, the researcher expressed her experience regarding honor and was able to hold her assumptions, beliefs, and biases at bay for the duration of the interviews. This allowed the researcher to be open to the participants' meanings and experience of the phenomenon. To reduce concerns, self-reflexivity was a continual part of the research process to reduce the influence of bias. In addition, the researcher practiced self-awareness throughout the heuristic process as to minimize researcher bias.

In regards to the researcher's sensitivity during interviews, it was found that by the time the interviews had begun the researcher's sensitivity had declined in part. This decrease in sensitivity could have affected the data collection; however, the researcher practiced self-awareness throughout the process. The researcher's objectivity may have been affected when the researcher experienced emotions empathetic to those of the participants. The shared experience or similar language used could have distracted the researcher during the interview from deeper inquiry. However, the researcher practiced self-awareness throughout the process and was able to overcome sensitivity issues and empathic distraction.

Additionally, it was understood that the researcher might have misunderstood or distorted the data collected from participants due to bias or memory recall. However, the researcher circumvented that issue by audio recording all interview and taking field notes at the end of interviews. Therefore, the researcher through the recordings, eliminating any misheard, distorted, or biased data, can verify the collected data.

As previously stated, the understanding of heuristic research is that there is no hypothesis. Rather, that the expected findings of the study will reveal themselves to the researcher as the research questions are explored through the data. The role of the researcher is not to prove or disprove, but to illustrate the experience of the participants and their own experiences regarding the research questions. It was expected that the heuristic process of inquiry would lead to a creative synthesis of the lived experience of honor among Arab American women.

Organization of the Remainder of the Study

Chapter 1 presents an overview of the proposed study. The subsequent chapters present the information collected in conjunction with this study. Chapter 2 provides the literature review, which includes an overview of research involving Islam, Women in Islam, American Islam, Immigration and Assimilation of Arab Americans, Honor, and Honor Killings. Chapter 3 presents details about the heuristic inquiry methodology that was used to collect the data in this study. Chapter 4 presents the data analysis conducted by the researcher. Chapter 5 contains the results and discussion of the study, as well as recommendations for any future research on related topics.

CHAPTER 2. LITERATURE REVIEW

Introduction to the Literature Review

This study explored the lived experience of honor among Levantine first generation Arab American women. The significance of this topic arose out of the increased research in Arab culture, Arab women, current affairs in the Arab world, and Arab religion(s). There is an increase in research on Arab women regarding honor killings, and while the primary researcher's interest was peaked by the occurrence of honor killings, they were not the focus of this study. Rather, the phenomenon of honor as an experience was the focus. That being said, there is a gap in research regarding honor itself and how it applies to Arab American women in the United States. Areas of study that contribute to research regarding the lived experience of honor among Levantine first generation Arab American women include research on Islam, women and Islamic culture, the Arab American communities and their assimilation into American culture and honor from an anthropological perspective. It is imperative that these topics be understood to realize how the lived experience of honor affects Levantine first generation Arab American women.

This study took form following an extensive literature review of research related to Islam, Muslim Women, honor killings, the Arab American experience, and heuristic phenomenology. The literature review utilized the libraries of Capella University and Iona College. Various databases were explored including PsycARTICLES (EBSCOhost),

Sage Psychology Collection, EBSCO, and Dissertations and Theses Full Text (ProQuest).

Key Words such as "Islam," "Muslim women," "honor," "honor killings," "Arab

American," "Arab women," "Quran," "Quran and women," "assimilation,"

"acculturation," "qualitative," "heuristic inquiry," "heuristic phenomenology," and

"phenomenology" were utilized to explore the subject.

This chapter provides the framework needed to understand the gap in the

literature regarding the lived experience of honor among Levantine Arab American

women. It also provides an understanding of the related issues and phenomena, as they

are deeply intertwined. This chapter begins with a brief discussion about the beginnings

of Islam and the religion itself. It then discusses the role of women in regards to Islamic

culture. As part of this discussion, an explanation of interpretation of sacred text, as

relevant to the female perspective, takes place. Furthermore, given the recent research on

Arab immigration patterns into the United States, a brief introduction, and explanation of

Arab American communities and assimilation is discussed. It then discusses the concept

of honor as it has been researched from an anthropological perspective. Lastly, the

significance of taking a heuristic approach towards gaining an understanding of the lived

experience of honor among Levantine first generation Arab American women is

discussed, and how this study addresses a gap in the current literature. This section

concludes with a summary of the chapter.

Theoretical Orientation for the Study

Theoretical orientation develops as various paths to understanding about how an

individual's problems develop and how the problems can be solved. The concepts

regarding the development of problems are called theoretical orientation, which is the guiding principle in developing a treatment plan for the individual or issue. One

theoretical orientation that is utilized in regards to Arab Americans is family therapy.

This is especially relevant due to the waves of immigration from the Middle East; there is

a growing and substantial Arab population in the United States (D'Agostino, 2002). This

growing population, like any other, has mental health issues. Psychologists, social

workers, and other mental health workers need to become culturally competent in order

to assist Arab Americans and their mental health needs. Research that assists in the

cultural competence has increased over the years.

As immigrant populations have increased, the need for cultural competency in

mental health workers, psychologists, social workers, etc., has also increased. The

population that these professions are interacting with is ever changing therefore, the

theories of culture and psychology that applies to one may not apply to another. Sam and

Berry (2010) proposed that those who work in the mental health profession might

increase their cultural competency by completing the following steps in understanding

the process of acculturation. The first is to understand what acculturation is;

"acculturation entails a variety of processes and outcomes; groups and individuals within

groups adopt different ways to deal with the acculturation experience" (Sam & Berry,

2010, p. 473). When the researcher understands that it is both a group and individual

process, the researcher is able to comprehend the impact on both the group and

individual. In addition, there needs to be an understanding of the impact the groups and

individuals have on each other during the process of acculturation. Next, there needs to

be an understanding of the original cultures before they encounter with one another. Sam

and Berry (2010) discussed it as follows, "Acculturating individuals and groups bring cultural and psychological qualities with them to the new society, and the new society also has a variety of such qualities" (p. 473).

Following this understanding of the two original cultures, there needs to be an understanding of all the forms of changes that occur during acculturation. Sam and Berry (2010) stressed a three-step approach to understanding the changes occurring during acculturation, "a stress and coping theoretical framework, a culture learning approach, and a social-identification orientation to acculturation" (p. 474). The process of acculturation is a life change that is stressful for the individual and as such, the individual develops coping mechanisms to deal with the stressors. This is handled differently for different individuals; some handle the stress of acculturation better than others do. In this instance, a cultural competent mental health counselor, psychologist, or social worker may be very helpful during this process. In regards to a culture learning approach, this is the process in which the individual learns to interact within their new culture. Sam and Berry (2010) described it as "the starting point is to identify cross-cultural differences in communication (both verbal and nonverbal), rules, conventions, norms, and practices that contribute to intercultural misunderstandings" (p. 477). Figuring out social norms, greetings, and interactions can not only greatly reduce the stress of acculturation, but can also speed up the process of acculturation for the individual. Lastly, a social identification orientation to acculturation is needed. The individual may choose to either orient themselves towards their new culture without engaging their former culture. Another approach is to orient themselves towards new culture while engaging their former culture. Sam and Berry (2010) discussed this preference as dependent on the ethnic group.

Citing a 2006 study of Sam and Berry (2010), the authors explained,

Separation appeared to be the most preferred strategy (40.3%) for the combined Turkish samples (*n*=714). In contrast, those in the Vietnamese sample (*n*=718) seemed to prefer assimilation (25.6%) nearly as much as integration (33.1%), and these preferences were related to whether the Vietnamese resided in a "settler society" (p. 477).

Daneshpour (1998), Dwairy (1997), and Smith (2011) have written extensively on cultural understanding in regards to the Arab American population that the mental health population is now meeting. Daneshpour (1998) focused on the application of family therapy methods to Arab and Muslim families. There is an emphasis on the difference in the value systems between the two cultures. It was found that the Arab and Muslim family preference was for "for greater connectedness, a less flexible and more hierarchical family structure, and an implicit communication style" (Daneshpour, 1998, p. 355). Dwairy (1997) also covered the techniques used to treat Arab and Muslim patients. His research focused on the needs of the client based on the practice in Arab culture that the needs of the family come before the needs of the individual. Smith (2011) focused his research on the Arab Americans who would not utilize mental health services and how to remove the cultural barriers and stigma around mental health assistance. Regarding conflicts between Islam and therapy, fear of stigma, preference to spiritually focused healing, and mistrust of mental health workers, Smith (2011) discussed the reasoning why Arab immigrants and their children would choose not to get assistance for mental health issues.

When discussing the issues of immigration of Arab people to the United States, acculturation theory is an essential part of the conversation. Berry (2005), discussed the two levels at which acculturation occurs, "At the group level, it involves changes in social structures and institutions and in cultural practices. At the individual level, it involves changes in a person's behavioral repertoire" (p. 699). The process of acculturation is not one that occurs quickly. Rather, it is a lengthy and sometimes generational process. The participants in this study are first generation and therefore, are sometimes in the midst of the process. This can cause friction in familial and personal relationships, which are made clear in the interview process. Berry (2005) also discussed the strategies that can be utilized during the acculturation process, focusing on either of two perspectives, "These issues involve the distinction between (1) a relative preference for maintaining one's heritage culture and identity, and (2) a relative preference for having contact with and participating in the larger society along with other ethno-cultural groups" (p. 704). In the study, it is seen that the first generation women participants are of the second group. These women would prefer to participate in American culture and society. Their parents, the immigrant generation, are of the first group, who would prefer to maintain their original culture and preserve their ethnic identity.

Review of Research Literature Specific to the Topic

Islam: A Brief Summary

To understand the lived experience of the Levantine Arab American women, it is essential to understand the religion of Islam, which is the religion of the majority in the Levant. Islam is the world's fastest growing religion, the second largest, and the youngest of the monotheistic faiths (Judaism, Christianity, and Islam). Over 1.5 billion people on the planet identify themselves religiously as Muslims (Hamid, 2008). While Islam is sternly monotheistic (the belief in one God), it is certainly not monolithic. Islam is practiced differently in every country, culture, and region where the religion has spread. While the language of the Quran is classical Arabic, only 19% of Muslims are Arabic language speakers, leaving 81% of the world's Muslims speaking a variety of other languages. Islam as a religion is not only diverse in where is it practiced, but also how it is practiced. Each community, culture, or region that adopts the Islamic faith has adapted the faith to each specific community. With awareness of this heterogeneity, it is wise to adopt a broad understanding of the Islamic faith and the Muslim thought process in general. Hamid (2008) warned the scholar to avoid the narrow approach to the understanding of Islam in practice, therefore isolating the interpretation and understanding of the religion. It is at this point in the discussion that Islam is not a monolithic practice, and it is helpful to look at Islam from a historical perspective.

The Islamic faith was established by the Prophet Mohammed in the pre-Islamic Arabian Peninsula in 610 AD with the first revelation from the Arch Angel Gabriel (Hamid, 2008; Zentella, 2010). The Prophet Mohammed was born and raised in the city of Mecca, in current day Saudi Arabia, and was a member of the *Quraysh* tribe. The *Quraysh* tribe was the maintainer of the *Kaaba* at this point. The *Kaaba*, which is now an Islamic Holy site, has always been a site of commercialism and pilgrimage and was kept in order by the *Quraysh* tribe. During his adult life, Mohammed would often steal away to the mountains of Mecca, meditate and practice calming techniques. It was at this point in this life when he was about 40 that he received his first revelation from *Allah* or God. Delivered by the Arch Angel Gabriel, this vision and revelation were Mohammed's first of the many religious messages he would receive. These religious messages called

Mohammed to instruct all mankind to worship the one and true God. The messages were delivered in the form of classical Arabic, which is in the form of high Arabic poetry (Hamid, 2008). These revelations, as they were recited to Mohammed by Gabriel and by Mohammed to the Muslim community, were later organized into the *Quran*. The *Quran* is the sacred text of Islam, with 113 *Surahs*, or verses, and 500 pages. This sacred text is the foundation for the belief system of Muslims (Hamid, 2008).

As Mohammed preached the newly revealed religion of Islam to the peoples of the Arabian Peninsula, he had much success. All people, from the slaves of the city of Mecca to the aristocrats of the city of Mecca were drawn to the charismatic Mohammed and his new religion. There were those who were not interested in this new faith, one that put a priority on submission to Allah and less priority on tribal hierarchy. The higher up tribal leaders in Mecca were threatened by Mohammed and his religion, which had quite the following. Eventually, the resentment of the tribal authorities drove Mohammed to leave Mecca and move to Medina. This migration is called the *Hijra* and is considered the official start of the Islamic calendar (Hamid, 2008). Once Mohammed and his followers settled in Medina, they set about establishing the foundations of the Islamic faith. Social, civil, and legal issues were all regulated according to values put forth in the Quran. The group identified themselves as the *Ummah*, the Islamic community. During this time of establishment, Mohammed utilized his charisma and persuasive powers to unite the group from a disorganized pack of believers to a united, structured community. This shift from "an oppressed marginalized cult to a growing religious community and influential political entity" is why Islam was able to flourish in the region and beyond (Hamid, 2008, p. 8). Muslims are urged to live their lives using the Prophet Mohammed as a model. Mohammed is described as "the most balanced and perfect human being" (Hamid, 2008, p. 6). They are also expected to learn not only from the *Quran* but also from the *Sunnah*, which is a collection of Mohammed's teachings and sayings, a guide on how to live your life as the Prophet did (Zentella, 2010).

After the death of Mohammed, there was an invested interest in the preservation of the Prophet's teachings and an expansion of those teachings into law. This development of Islamic law, known as *Sharia*, is considered the constitution of the Islamic faith (Zentella, 2010). The development of Sharia was to put into place a series of laws that regulated the social, civil, and religious life of the *Ummah*. Sharia is based on the law created from interpretations from the revelations in the Quran primarily. A secondary source of Sharia is the *Hadith*, the sayings and teachings of the Prophet collected by believers and documented by his companions (Hamid, 2008). These sacred texts, the Quran, Sunnah, Hadith, and Sharia all inform the way of life of the Muslim individual. The texts inform, regulate, and control the actions, thoughts, culture, and mentality of each Muslim individual. It is important to understand the evolution of the religion of Islam, its laws, and its customs. Islam informs the life of the believer in every aspect publically, privately, mentally, and socially.

Women in Islam: An Overview

It would be difficult to begin the discussion regarding women in Islam without firstly reviewing the work of Leila Ahmed, specifically her book, *Women and Gender in Islam: Historical Roots of a Modern Debate* (Ahmed, 1992). Ahmed reviewed the role of women in pre-Islamic history as well as Islamic history and focused on the changing role of women in Islam as time moves forward. There is a distinguishing between the gender roles that were already in place in pre-Islamic times and the gender roles that are in place today. Utilizing anthropological and theological resources, Ahmed identified the cultural and religious influences that have shaped the role of Arab and Muslim women in Arab society today. Another valuable resource regarding women and gender in Islam is Beck and Keddie's (1980) *Women in the Muslim World*. While the text is a bit older in comparison to other resources, it is one of the foundational and first resources to cover women in the Muslim world, country by country. Beck and Keddie surveyed the role of women in Morocco, Turkey, Tunisia, Algeria, Kuwait, Iran, Egypt, Syria, Lebanon, Pakistan, and North Africa. Each country is reviewed by the socioeconomic and legal position of women, the historical role of women, and the role of religion and ritual. The works focus on motherhood, childbirth, and most importantly virginity. The main message of the series is that the terms virginity and female have categorical importance when discussing women, their role in the world, and their role in Islam.

Shifting from the anthropological perspective to the theological one, Barlas' (2002) work *Believing Women in Islam*, is a resource that addresses Muslims and non-Muslims, men and women, regarding sacred text. The main question throughout the text is whether the Quran is a patriarchal text. In addition, Barlas challenges the Muslim woman to re-read the Quran from an egalitarian perspective. It is in the initial reading of the text from a patriarchal perspective that allows the Muslim woman to stop and open the door for the "liberating and egalitarian voice of Islam" (Barlas, 2002, p. 4). Amina Wadud's (1999) work, *Qur'an and Woman: Rereading the Sacred Text from a Woman's Perspective,* is also research from the theological perspective. For the non-Muslim reader, this text is an informative resource regarding Muslim women engaging in the traditionally considered male practice of *Tafsir,* or Quranic commentary. Quranic commentary is a review, evaluation, summarization, and explanation of sacred text. Wadud explained that her book is less about Muslim women and more about the concept of women in the Quran, read by women, from the woman's perspective. Wadud's work establishes gender equality and finds supportive statements in the Quran having read it from the female perspective, which at the time of publishing was a novel idea.

Moving towards the psychological perspective of the literature, Sabbah's (1984) work *Women in the Muslim Unconscious* is the foundational work regarding Islam, women, and their bodies. There is a focus on the concept of the Islamic female ideal being passive, silent, and obedient. There is also a focus on the other side of the ideal Islamic woman coin that she is overly sexualized and reduced to a sexual object. Sabbah's work discussed the painful reality of shoving an individual, in this case, Arab and Muslim women, into one role or the other, which prevents them from fulfilling their potential as human beings. This reality is described as erotic discourse, in which the individual's responsibilities and abilities are reduced down to their sexuality, and empowers the opposite sex. She boils the Quran, Sunnah, Hadith, and Sharia down to displaying "woman as an object of pleasure and the product of male sacred power" (Sabbah, 1984, p. 112). The woman and her sexuality are so important to the understanding of male power that misogyny becomes the norm. Sabbah also does not exclusively hold men as the oppressors of women, rather is it the Muslim order (as supported by the Quran, Sunnah, Hadith, Sharia, and Tafsir) that do not allow the male or female believers to fulfill their full potential. Rather, they are imprisoned by their gender roles, as they are laid out in the sacred texts.

Immigration and Assimilation

In researching any nationality or ethnicity and the corresponding immigration patterns, one will find that there are always rushes and droughts in immigration to the United States. Michael Suleiman (1999) presented the immigration patterns of Arabs and Muslims to the United States in his book *Arabs in America: Building a New Future*. Suleiman dates the first waves of Arab immigration to the United States beginning as early as the middle of the 18th century. Most were Christians and were almost all categorized as "Turks," as there was little understanding at that point regarding the various nationalities that made up the Middle East. Another increased wave of immigration of Arabs to the United States occurred after World War I. These immigrants were labeled at this point "Arabians." The third wave of Arab immigration to the United States is dated at its highest between 1945-1960. While there is still a constant flow of immigration from Arab countries, legislation in recent years has restricted the flow somewhat. Currently, Arab and Muslim immigrants live throughout the United States and are often concentrated in urban areas, mainly on either the East or West coasts (Haddad, 1991). The two most concentrated states in regards to Arab and Muslims immigrants are New York and California; one-quarter of the nation's Arabs and Muslims live in New York, and one-fifth live in California (Kosmin & Lachman, 1993).

Yvonne Haddad (2011), a foundational researcher of the Arab American experience, has not only researched the immigration patterns of Arabs to the United States but has dedicated her career to understanding the assimilation of the Arab immigrant. The transition from Arab immigrant to Arab American is one documented in her book *Becoming American?:The Forging of Arab and Muslim Identity in Pluralist*

America. By documenting the waves of immigration, covering American Muslim of note, and reviewing the first documentation of Muslims in America, she has given the reader a comprehensive history of the immigration and assimilation of the Arab American Muslim. Haddad found that for Muslims to assimilate more easily, two things were needed. The first was for the establishment of community centers and mosques. This allowed for immigrant Arab Muslims to have a home base. The second thing needed for easy assimilation was an *Imam* (Muslim spiritual leader) who was supportive and progressive in regards to assimilation into American culture.

Once these newly immigrated Muslims established communities and mosques, assimilation into American culture could begin. Duderija (2008) covered the conflicts of identity Western-born Muslims may have in his article *Literature Review: Identity Construction in the Context of Being a Minority Immigrant Religion: The Case of Western-born Muslims.* He discussed the shift from being a religious majority in their homeland to a now minority in their new land. The shift can cause a crisis of identity and faith. Those crises can become more apparent in the first generation children of these immigrant individuals. The children of these Arab immigrants are often quick to assimilate and this can cause friction in the family. One of the first works to cover the traits of the assimilated Arab American woman and their experience is Shakir's (1997) book, *Bint Arab: Arab and Arab American Women in the United States.* Shakir is the first generation daughter of Arab American immigrants. Shakir's work focused primarily on Lebanese women and focused on first, second, and third-generation Arab American women. The work is divided into several parts where two are quite informative regarding the Arab American woman's experience regarding assimilation. The first focuses on the excitement of the immigrant women living in a new country. The second focuses on the ease and difficulties of the first generation's assimilation. In addition, it focuses on the revival of interest in ethnic heritage that occurred in the second and third generations. Shakir gives several women the spotlight in her book, focusing on the constantly changing perspective of what it means to be Arab, what it means to be American, and what it means to be a woman in this community.

The Arab American immigrants that have traveled from their homes abroad have brought with them a culture, religion, and customs in which psychologists may have been unfamiliar. In order to understand how to treat individuals from this region, psychologists studied the immigrants, their families, and customs to gain a better understanding as to the needs and issues of the Arab American clientele. Understanding the adult Arab American requires psychologists to go back to adolescence and childhood. Timimi (1995) covered the mental health needs of the Arab American teenager, focusing on the problems of those teens from immigrant Arab families. There is an emphasis on the importance of the role and responsibility of the family in Arab American culture as well as the attitudes towards and the importance placed on female sexuality. Timimi also focused on the individual's transition from one culture to another, from Arab to American, and the conflicts (internal and external, individual and familial) that emerge as a result. Dwairy (1997) also covered the mental health issues of the Arab American client, however did not focus on a certain age. There is a focus on the role of the family in Dwairy's research, on how the family conditions the individual to behave, think, and feel. Dwairy posed that the Arab family structure and gender roles suppress the individual's sense of self, making the individual identify with the family unit. By doing so, there is a suppression of the self-actualization of the individual. There is a focus on the group, not self. All actions, thoughts, and feelings are based on the greater good of the group (family) not the individual (self). If an individual's actions are so important in regards to how the group (family) is perceived, logically the individual's thoughts, feelings and most importantly actions would be tightly controlled. To sum up, the needs of the individual are secondary to the needs of the family, which is contradictory to American culture and the American individual.

Honor

There are many definitions of what constitutes honor. However, for this study the definition discussed by Frank Henderson Stewart (1994) is utilized. Anthropologist Frank Henderson Stewart (1994) discussed honor as having two components, "One is 'objectified honor', which is a person's good reputation, the other 'subjectified honor', is a person's sense of their self-worth" (p. 34). Objectified honor holds much weight in the sense that there is significance in what others think about us. The society in which one lives dictates a person's social worth. This is different from subjectified honor, in which an individual determines their self-worth. While there is sufficient literature on honor itself, there is little to no literature on the lived experience of honor (Stewart, 1994). As previously discussed, researchers such as Dwairy (1997), have found that the individual's wants, needs, and actions in the Arab American family unit are often minimized and suppressed for the greater good and image of the whole Arab American family unit. There is a sense that the thoughts, feelings, and actions of the individual can bring on either a good or a bad reputation. However, when discussing honor, it would appear the latter, actions, are the most damning of the three to tarnish the reputation of the Arab American family unit.

It is important to note the role of religion in this dynamic. Immigrants that come from Arab countries bring with them culture, customs, and religion. Fadia Faqir (2001) wrote that the role of Islam and religion in general takes a back seat to the tribal concepts of honor, "Societal and political structures conspire to form a parallel system, which is stronger than the Islamic religion" (p. 1). Therefore, the protection of one's tribal or familial honor takes precedence over the actual Islamic teachings. The reason the concept of honor is so highly valued and the practices that result from the high value are not contested officially is that the Muslim and Middle Eastern identity that the people of the region value so, is constantly being threatened (whether the threat is real or not) by Western influence. To keep their culture, which is a compilation of religion and culture, they must keep their women pure and their society clean of any type of western influence. Western influence includes women having premarital sex, women having children out of wedlock, and women dressing in an immodest way. The fear of Western influence comes not from the religious aspect but from a political one. For centuries, the British and the French colonized parts of the Middle East, creating their own subculture within the occupied states. The reaction to the colonization and the changing society towards a more modern society created an increase in Islamization of the people of the occupied state. The ones who suffer from an increase in religious law and enforcement of tribal customs are the women. However, one can follow the cause and reaction that creates this need for attachment to one's culture and faith in the face of occupation as a form of political resistance.

What happens when an individual chooses Western influence? What happens when an individual chooses to honor their own thoughts and feelings as opposed to those of the family? It is the (non-conforming, non-family value focused) actions of these individuals that are often cited as the catalyst of the honor killing of that individual. An honor killing occurs when a female family member has dishonored or shamed her family by participating in a reputation-damaging behavior, situation, or association with a dishonorable person. To cleanse the family's honor (allowing the remaining females to marry into respectable families), the dishonorable female is killed, usually by a male family member (Kulczycki & Windle, 2011). Rana Husseini (2009) discussed the honor killings that are occurring specifically in the country of Jordan, including motives, methods, and family backgrounds. Husseini is a well-known reporter in Jordan who was the first to profile several men who have committed honor killings in Jordan. Her compilation of interviews, family stories, individual stories (men and women) is informative regarding why this phenomenon is occurring. By interviewing both the women who are victims of the phenomenon and the men who commit the honor killings, Husseini is enabling the understanding of both sides. She finds that there is intense pressure for Arab men and women in regards to honor. The common pattern in all the cases profiled is the societal and familial pressures placed on the individuals in these families.

Methodological Literature

Honor

Honor has been researched in regards to insult and defense of honor, usually from the male perspective (Leung & Cohen, 2011). In these experimental studies, the participant is insulted in some way, ranging from a bump or verbal insult. The participant's honor is now tarnished unless they retaliate to regain it. Cohen, Nisbett, Bowdle, and Schwartz (1996) researched the "culture of honor" in the American South. An experiment was conducted comparing participants' reactions to being bumped and insulted. Participants were from the North and the South. It was found that Southern participants were more likely to view their honor as threatened by the bump and insult and more likely to respond violently. In the study conducted by Leung and Cohen (2011), the researchers analyzed the concept of within and between cultures, meaning an individual may or may not reject cultural rules when honor is being threatened. In this study, the researchers set up various situations for participants where they were prepared to either pay back an insult or pay back a favor. In situations where the participant was set up to pay back a favor, the participant was more likely to pay back the favor if the participant spent face-to-face time with the confederate to whom the favor was owed. In situations where the participant was set up to pay back an insult, it was found that the participants who were from the American South or Hispanic were more likely to utilize or endorse violence to redeem their honor.

Similarly, there is also a culture of honor in the Arab and Arab American communities. Until more recently, these familial homicides have been classified as just that. Phyllis Chesler (2010) utilized a correlational study researched the patterns and

38

themes of the increase in intra-familial violence and femicide. Utilizing an in-depth look at the inner workings of these communities, law enforcement has identified trends and patterns in these violent crimes, for females and honor. Chesler found that the enforcement of honor is not only a male/female dynamic but also an individual/familial one.

A quantitative study regarding the attitudes of adolescents in Amman, Jordan towards honor killings was conducted by Eisner and Ghuneim (2013) from the United Kingdom. This study is relevant though not having been conducted in the United States, as there has not been a study in this vein yet conducted in the U.S. The researchers distributed questionnaires to 856 ninth graders in a secondary school in Amman, Jordan. The participants were between the ages of 14 and 16 and there were 455 female and 401 male participants. It was found that boys were more than twice as likely as girls to endorse or approve of honor killings. In addition, it was concluded that "Amongst adolescents from the lowest level of educational background 61% endorsed at least two honor killing attitudes, while this was the case for only 21.1% of the adolescents where at least one family member has a university degree" (Eisner & Ghuneim, 2013, p. 7). In light of these findings, it was found that individuals from more traditional backgrounds were more likely to approve of honor killings.

In a qualitative study regarding virginity, a researcher utilized the phenomenological approach to understand the importance of virginity from the perspective of the Arab American female. As mentioned earlier in the literature review, the findings of Rana Husseini indicated that a loss of virginity, or even suspected loss, was reason enough to incite a family member to honor kill the offending female family member. Therefore, a study on the concept of virginity from the perspective of the Arab American female is relevant. According to the three narratives showcased in the study, the researcher was able to understand that the individual's virginity was not only their own, but in a sense belonged to the community. The three major themes that emerged were Virginity as Identity, Embodiment of Virginity and "We are Arabs" (Abboud, 2014). For the participants, virginity defined the women. Virginity was a physical component to their physical being. Lastly, virginity was ethnically important, culturally important, and religiously important.

Acculturation

As the co-researchers in this study are first generation Arab American, it is important to take into consideration the process of acculturation the participants have had to go through. Faragallah, Schumm, and Webb (1997) conducted an exploratory study regarding the acculturation process of Arab American Immigrants. The research hypothesis for this exploratory study was that "identification and acculturation may not imply satisfaction with the new culture or particularly satisfaction with family life within the new culture" (Faragallah, Schumm, & Webb, 1997, p. 183). The independent variables in this study included; exposure to U.S. culture, age at immigration, traditionalism, and discrimination. The dependent variable was satisfaction with live in America.

The participants recruited for this study were adult males, who were married, who had recently immigrated to the United States. Data from participants was gathered from Missouri, Indiana, Florida, Maryland, New York, Kansas, Pennsylvania, and California. The researchers collected data from these participants via mailed survey, asking questions

40

regarding; income, attendance to religious services, full or part time employment, language used in the home, identification with American culture, American media usage, marital satisfaction, family life satisfaction, and satisfaction with life. It was found that the longer the participant resided in the United States and the longer it had been since they had visited their home country, the more acculturated they were to American culture. In addition, it was found that "with greater acculturation to U.S. society was greater satisfaction with U.S. life, but with reduced family satisfaction" (Faragallah, Schumm, & Webb, 1997, p. 197). The issue of acculturation and mental health of Arab Americans comes into play in the following study in this methodological literature review.

In the correlational study by Aprahamian, Kaplan, Windham, Sutter, and Visser (2011), the goal was to measure the relationship between acculturation and mental health. It was hypothesized by the researchers that the more acculturated the participant was, the better their mental health. The participants were pulled from three Detroit counties. The sample consisted of 466 males and 538 females, between the ages of 13 and 70. Of the participants, 279 were born in the United States and of those who were not, "238 were from Iraq, 227 from Lebanon, 71 from Yemen, 52 from Palestine, 37 from Jordan, 30 from Egypt, 28 from Syria, 13 from Kuwait, 6 from Saudi Arabia, 2 from United Arab Emirates, and 25 from other regions; 8 responses were missing" (Aprahamian et al., 2011, p. 84). The researchers utilized The Kessler Psychological Distress Scale to measure mental health and the Marin and Marin Acculturation Scale to measure acculturation. The KIO is "a 10-item self-report questionnaire measuring nonspecific psychological distress" (Aprahamian et al., 2011, p. 84). The Marin and Marin

Acculturation Scale "consists of 12 closed-ended items utilizing a five-point response scale. Respondents are asked for their preference with which they perform certain behaviors (i.e., language usually spoken at home, preference of the ethnicity of people at social gatherings, etc.)" (Marin, Marin, Sabogal, Otero-Sabogal, & Perez-Stable, 1987, p. 187). Multiple linear regression analyses were used to determine the association between mental health and acculturation. The more acculturated the individual was it did not determine that the individual was in good mental health.

Mental Health

In the discussion of mental health and Arab Americans, one study that is important to note is Aloud and Rathur's (2009) exploratory, descriptive-associational study titled *Factors Affecting Attitude Toward Seeking and Using Formal Mental Health and Psychological Services Among Arab Muslim Populations*. The sample included participants from "five Islamic organizations providing religious, social, political, and educational services within Columbus, Ohio" (Aloud & Rathur, 2009, p. 80). Using questionnaires distributed through these organizations, the researcher was able to collect 285 responses to the 360 surveys mailed out. The survey utilized by Aloud and Rathur (2009) included questions regarding

> a) attitudes toward seeking and using formal mental health/psychological services; b) cultural beliefs about mental health/psychological problems; c) knowledge about and 50 familiarity with formal mental health services; and d) a demographics sheet that also inquired about the potential sources of help Arab-Muslims might seek when experiencing mental health difficulties. (p. 82)

It was found that there were negative attitudes towards seeking and using mental health services. There were specific cultural beliefs regarding mental health issues, including possession, and limited familiarity with the mental health services in general. In fact, it was found that Arab Americans would rather utilize all informal methods of resolving mental health issues, such as family discussion or the involvement of an *Imam*, before utilizing a mental health professional or facility.

In regards to the involvement of an *Imam* in the area of mental health, there has been a study regarding the role of the religious leader in this situation. The Arab American concept of identity is a conflicted one. The newly immigrated Arabs may still identify as Arab whereas the first generation Arab Americans may not. There are studies that have been conducted regarding the concept of identity among Arab Americans, specifically a cross-sectional survey of 22 *Imams* in New York City, post 9/11. The study was able to recruit, via mail invitation to the study, 22 *imams* and 102 worshippers to survey the role of the Imam in the promotion of mental health in their mosque. The imams were given a questionnaire, which "was intended to ascertain the types of problems for which worshippers sought guidance and the methods used to help resolve these problems" (Abu-Ras, Gheith, & Cournos, 2008, p. 162). The worshippers were given a questionnaire that included questions regarding (Abu-Ras et al., 2008)

> general demographic variables; the role of imams as perceived by worshippers; the type of counseling sought at mosques for a variety of issues, such as marital problems, financial woes, child rearing, personal development, emotional problems, intergenerational conflicts, sexual problems, religious clarifications, and personal safety issues; changes in mosque attendance since 9/11; issues of confidentiality regarding personal information shared with imams; and whether or not personal problems were being adequately addressed by the imams. (p. 162)

The findings of this study confirm the previous study in that the worshippers were not likely to use the services of mental health services or professionals, and "while religion and spirituality are key elements of mental health treatment methods in the New York City Muslim community, they are also often the only ones available to this community" (Abu-Ras et al., 2008, p. 168). The *Imams* are usually the first contact when there is strife in the family; however, they are not trained in crisis counseling or know who to refer worshippers to in these situation. However, researchers found that "expressed great eagerness to learn Western psychotherapy methods of treatments, and believed in combining Islamic tradition with modern talk psychotherapy and medication as the most effective approach to treating people with emotional problems" (Abu-Ras et al., 2008, p. 168).

Identity

As the Muslim and Arab population has grown in the past few decades, the formation of a Muslim/Arab-American identity has also been emerging (Kayyali, 2005). Some of this population will identify with both Arab and American identity and this situation is explored in a mixed methods study by Sirin et al. (2008). The researchers took a closer look at the individual's relationship between their American identity and their Muslim Identity. Researchers collected data from 97 participants, 55 women and 42 men, between the ages of 18-28. Forty-four percent were first generation and 56% were second generation. The researchers used "used measures of identity (qualitative and quantitative), acculturation practices, religiosity, frequency of discrimination, discrimination-related stress, as well as a demographic questionnaire" (Sirin et al., 2008, p. 265). It was found that even though the participants did identify with their Muslim side of their identity, they were able to include their American identity into their collective identity. In addition, the researchers found two points:

> First, the components of Muslim and American collective identities were either positively correlated or independent from one another, which suggest biculturalism in Berry's (2006) conceptualization. Second, participants

overwhelmingly preferred engagement in social and cultural activities of both their ethnic and religious communities and the mainstream US society. (Sirin et al., 2008, p. 274)

These participants identify themselves as both American and Muslim. By being able to incorporate both aspects of their identities, these participants reduce the occurrence of discrimination related stress in their lives. Researchers also found that a majority of the participants did not report a conflict in the existence of the two identities.

In regards to qualitative studies in reference to identity, a dissertation titled *Constructing the collective experience of being Arab American in post-9/11 America,* gives a view into the lives of Arab Americans after 9/11 and how they identify themselves in a post 9/11 world. Using the methodology of auto ethnography, the researcher was able to use narrative to illustrate to the reader the experience of the Arab American in the post 9/11 world. The researcher covers Arab American narrative in regards to flying as an Arab American and how it is different to fly otherwise, being targeted in schools based solely on ethnicity and being bullied, political issues, and the third space of identity that some Arab Americans occupy. The third space is "We aren't really Arab, we don't live in predominantly Arab communities in the US and we don't speak Arabic. Many of us pass for White and some of us even come from European ancestry by way of a parent" (Mufdi, 2012, p. 146). This feeling of otherness was a common theme throughout the study and one the participants in this study also identified with.

An additional qualitative study, a descriptive study, the researcher aimed to describe the Arab American woman's experience of living in the United States. Using semi-structured interviews, the researcher aimed to gather as much information as she could regarding the lives of the participants living as Arab American women in the United States. It was found that there were several themes that emerged including "(1) Coping and embracing the good, (2) Hybrid positionality, (3) Safety through invisibility, (4) Spiritual growth and family bonding, and (5) Fear of the unknown future" (Khatib, 2013, p. 60). This study provided a descriptive narrative on Arab American women's experience in regards to daily life, challenges, feelings, and their behaviors in America.

Synthesis of the Research Findings

The articles used in this research present a clear background of the religion of Islam and the role of women in Islam. In reviewing the research findings, it is clear that the research on Islam as a religion are informative in regards to understanding the faith of a majority of Arabs and Arab Americans (Hamid, 2008; Zentella, 2010). Concepts of Islam are imperative to the understanding of the religion, culture, and practice of the participants of this study. It is just as important to understand the role of women in Islam. As the participants for the study are solely Levantine first generation Arab American women, it is imperative to have an understanding of the role of women in the context of religion. Islam is a religion that informs all aspects of the believer's life, down to the everyday details, therefore, it was critical to gain an understanding of the tenets of the Islamic faith as well as how those tenets are applied to women of the faith. Islam is a growing, monotheistic faith that subscribes to specific gender roles for men and women.

The articles used in this literature review agree regarding the influx of Arabs and Muslims into the United States, and due to that influx, there is a conflict in assimilation for the immigrants and first generation children of those immigrants (D'Agostino, 2002; Haddad, 1991). In addition, the articles reviewed in this literature highlight the role that honor plays in the lives of the Arab and Muslim immigrants that immigrate to the United States, and the roots of the concept of honor traced back to tribal communities (Bailey, 2009; Peristiany, 1965; Stewart, 1994). The concept of honor also ties into the literature reviewed in regards to personhood and the self and the family (Krause, 1995; Mauss, 1954). The importance of the wants and needs of community and family as more important than the needs and wants of the individual are highlighted throughout the literature and illustrate the validity and importance of these themes. The articles reviewed agree about the need for cultural competency for the effective treatment of Arab and Muslim clients. For treatment to be effective for the growing population of Arab and Muslim clients, psychologists have to be able to utilize therapeutic approaches that are positively received by this population. The articles reviewed agree to this utilization and outline which approaches have been received well by the Arab and Muslim clients (Dwairy, 1997; Hodge & Nadir, 2008).

Critique of the Previous Research

The largest limitation is that each of these studies researches a part of the larger picture regarding the lived experience of Levantine first generation Arab American women. However, there has not been a study of the phenomenon itself. The available literature has focused on several aspects of the Middle East and its peoples, the religion (Hamid, 2008; Zentella, 2010), the culture and customs (Barakat, 1993; Pryce-Jones, 1989), the familial hierarchies (Hopkins, 2001; Moghadam, 2004; Stack, 2001) the immigration patterns (D'Agostino, 2002; Haddad, 1991; Hassan, 2000; Kayyali, 2005; Nigem, 1986), the acculturation (Amer & Hovey, 2007; Haddad, 2011; Tannous, 1943), and research regarding the mental health needs of the Arab client (Aloud & Rathur, 2009;

Aprahamian, Kaplan, Windham, Sutter, & Visser, 2011).

There is also substantial research regarding the concept of honor regarding the

individual and in relation to different parts of the world (Abu-Odeh, 2010; Doğan, 2011;

Faqir, 2001; Husseini, 2009; Madek, 2005; Onal, 2008; Peristiany, 1965; Stewart, 1994)

The weakness of the previous studies is that have come before is that those studies have

left a gap in the literature regarding the experience of honor among first generation

Levantine Arab American women, a gap that this study fills. The proposed research

question of "What is the lived experience of honor among first generation Arab American

women?" will contribute to the existing literature and background information regarding

honor. There has recently been an increase in honor-related crimes against women in the

United States (Chesler, 2010). This increase is the reasoning behind this proposed study.

The researcher would like to understand the concept of honor as it is experienced by

Levantine Arab American women.

The existing research that contributes to this study is extensive in various topics,

to include Arab women and gender (Ahmed, 1992), Muslim women in the United States

(Beck & Keddie, 1978), Islam in America (Abdo 2006; Haddad, 2011, Hassan 2000), the

concept of honor (Stewart, 1994), and honor killing (Husseini, 2009). There is a gap in

the literature about researching the experience of honor. Utilizing previous research of

Arabs, Muslims, women, and the concept of honor, the researcher conducted a heuristic

study to fill the gap in the literature of the experience of honor among first generation

Levantine Arab American women. The goal of this study was to gain an in-depth

understanding of the experience of honor among Levantine Arab American women. This study contributes to the field of psychology in several ways. The lived experience aspect of the study will contribute to humanistic studies of the participants. In addition, the discussion in regards to the sense of self, self-worth, and community ties will also contribute to the current psychological literature. Third, the study will incorporate and contribute to various disciplines in the research method and findings. This study will provide information to future researchers regarding Arab or Muslim women and honor as it is experienced.

As shown in the reviewed methodological literature, there have been several quantitative in regards to Arab women; honor (Abboud, 2014; Chesler, 2010; Cohen, Nisbett, Bowdle, & Schwartz, 1996; Eisner & Ghuneim, 2013), acculturation (Aprahamian, Kaplan, Windham, Sutter, & Visser, 2011; Faragallah, Schumm, & Webb, 1997; Marin et al., 1987) and mental health (Abu-Ras, Gheith, & Cournos, 2008; Aloud & Rathur, 2009). There have been no qualitative studies conducted in regards to the lived experience of honor among first generation, Levantine, Arab American women. The literature reviews showed a number of dissertations on aspects of honor. The dissertation topics included a phenomenological study of honor as a system (Oprisko, 2011), a legal narrative of honor killing in Canada (Fateh, 2012), an auto-ethnographical study on the attitudes and beliefs surrounding honor killings in the United States (Shaikh, 2014), and an anthropological study of honor, kinship, and marriage (Fedida, 1984).

There has not been sufficient current research on the lived experience of honor, a concept that is at the root of the already existing research on honor, honor killings, the Arab American experience regarding identity, acculturation, and mental health. The existing studies fall short o describing the lived experience of honor among first generation, Levantine, Arab American women. This study focused on the lived experience of first generation, Levantine, Arab American women. Utilizing Moustakas' (1990) heuristic approach, the researcher was able to understand, at the deepest level, this human experience. By doing so, there is an expansion of the scientific community's understanding of this lived experience, which could bring about new perspectives and methods regarding this phenomenon and those who experience it.

Summary

From evaluating this comprehensive literature review of peer-reviewed journals and books, it is clear that there is much more to learn about the experience of honor among Levantine first generation Arab American women. The reviewed literature clearly supports the researcher's need for information on Islam, women in Islam, immigration and assimilation, honor (its tribal origins and current role in culture), and mental health needs of Arab and Muslim clients. However, there is a deficiency in the exploration of the lived experience of honor among Levantine first generation Arab American women.

Through a heuristic approach, the lived experience of honor among Levantine first generation Arab American women is illustrated, adding to the literature base of Islam, Islamic women, assimilated Muslims, and honor crimes. No heuristic research was found that specifically addresses the lived experience of honor among Levantine first generation Arab American women as defined in this study. Therefore, studying Levantine first generation Arab American women provides an opportunity to begin to understand the lived experience of honor.

CHAPTER 3. METHODOLOGY

Purpose of the Study

The primary purpose of this heuristic study is to describe and understand the lived experience of honor among first generation, Levantine, Arab American women. The secondary purpose of this study was to contribute to the psychological literature base related to honor. Specifically, this study's goal was to contribute to the literature regarding the lived experience of honor among Levantine Arab American women using Moustakas' (1990) heuristic inquiry. The research goal was to uncover the lived experience of honor among Levantine Arab American Women, ages 25-35, by interviewing Levantine Arab American women.

Despite the increased occurrence of honor killings in the United States, the effect of honor and the lived experience of honor are still poorly understood (Chesler, 2010). This lack of knowledge and understanding of the experience creates a gap in the literature and a need to study the emotional, psychological, social, spiritual, and behavioral aspects of honor. Although there are studies that have been conducted that have explored related topics, these studies have not studied the lived experience of honor as it is experienced by first generation, Levantine, Arab American women (Abdo, 2006; Abu-Odeh, 2010; Bailey, 2009; Boosahda. 2003; Chesler, 2010; Faqir, 2001; Gilmore, 1987; Haddad, 1991, 2011; Hassan, 2000; Husseini, 2009; Madek, 2005; Peristiany & Pitt-Rivers, 1992; Peristiany, 1965; Stewart, 1994).

The research question was "What is the lived experience of honor among Levantine Arab American Women?" This research question is compatible with heuristic inquiry, in that heuristics allows the researcher to take an experience and fully illustrate it to those who do not experience the phenomenon. In addition, the researcher also is fluent in the experience. The researcher is a Levantine, first generation, Arab American women who has an intense interest and an intense experience with the phenomenon being studied. The intense experience and interest in the phenomenon allow heuristics inquiry to be the appropriate choice for methodology.

Research Design

Methodology: Heuristic Inquiry

The qualitative methodology used for this study is Moustakas' (1990) heuristic research. The goal of heuristic inquiry is to illuminate the lived experience of honor among first generation, Levantine, Arab American women. Intensity sampling was used and ensured that the participants were able to give vivid descriptions of the experience and illuminate the experience of honor. All the co-researchers and the primary researcher had first-hand experience with the phenomenon being studied. As the primary researcher's experience is also included in the study, there was a strict protocol to be followed regarding the process of heuristic inquiry.

The first concept in the protocol of heuristic inquiry is for the researcher to identify the focus of inquiry. Moustakas (1990) asks that the primary researcher fully immerse themselves in the research question. It is a requirement that the primary researcher has first-hand experience with the phenomenon being studied. The second concept in the protocol of heuristic inquiry is self-dialogue. In this step, the primary researcher is recognizing and documenting her connection with the phenomenon being studied. The primary researcher is documenting her experience with the phenomenon by completing her interview questions verbally and in journal form. Next, the primary researcher utilized the concept of tacit knowing. According to Polyani (1966), tacit knowledge is information that is in its whole form, greater than its divided parts. By collecting information from multiple participants in multiple ways allows the primary researcher to collect information regarding the experience from various perspectives and directions. In utilizing the next concept within heuristic inquiry, the primary researcher uses indwelling to turn "inward to seek a deeper, more extended comprehension of the nature or meaning of a quality or theme of human experience" (Moustakas, 1990, p. 24). At this point, the primary researcher will focus on any experience in the data collected that enhances the understanding of the experience.

Focusing in heuristic inquiry is a concept that allows the primary researcher to acknowledge and understand which parts of the data collected are shared in her own experience and which are not. By doing so, the primary researcher can focus on the emergent and shared themes in the data collected. The last protocol that is required for heuristic inquiry is the constant referral back to the internal frame of reference. Moustakas (1990) stated "To know, and understand the nature, meaning and essences of any human experience, one depends on the internal frame of reference of the person who has had, is having or will have the experience" (p. 26). The primary researcher has to refer to her internal frame of reference to understand the experience of the co-researchers.

These concepts in the heuristic protocol allow the researcher to participate fully in the six phases of heuristic research.

The researcher utilized Moustakas' (1990) six phases of Heuristic research; initial engagement, immersion, incubation, illumination, explication, and creative synthesis to access data, immerse herself in the data, and analyze the data. During the initial engagement, the researcher discovered the deep interest in the topic. Within the second step of immersion, the researcher surrounded herself with the research question and data. During the incubation period, the researcher took a step back after being fully involved in the research question, data collected, and related material (field notes, journals). The researcher moved on to illumination. It is in the fourth stage of illumination, the researcher has a breakthrough regarding the research question, the data collected, and the experience. In the following step of explication, the researcher examines what has surfaced as a result of the previous three stages (during immersion, incubation, and illumination). Finally, the last stage is creative synthesis. In this period of heuristic inquiry, the researcher was able to pull together the themes and patterns that have emerged into a descriptive and illustrative narrative regarding the experience of the co-researchers and the primary researcher.

Sample Type

The co-researchers in this heuristic study were female adults, between the ages of 25-35. These co-researchers have responded to a recruitment flyer for the study conducted, specifically focused on the lived experience of honor. The co-researchers were from the researcher's home community of an urban area in the North East and chosen by distributing flyers for the study in local Muslim communities. The researcher asked for willing participants for the study. Any individuals who contacted the researcher for the study was considered a volunteer and was chosen to participate in the study on a voluntary basis. There was no preference based on race, education, religion, social or economic status, or sexual orientation. However, to be a participant, volunteers have to be female, between the ages of 25 and 35, and be ethnically from the Levant in the Middle East.

The larger population from which the sample of co-researchers of the study was drawn from were Arab American Women in the United States. The target population for this study was first generation, Levantine, Arab American women. Criteria for selecting the co-researchers included (1) women from the Levant in the Middle East which includes; Lebanon, Syria, Jordan, Egypt, Palestinian territories, and Israel; (2) co-researchers may be single or married; (3) the co-researchers must be first generation American citizens, one or both parents may have immigrated to the United States; (4) the co-researchers are to be between the ages of 25 and 35.

Data Collection

The researcher conducted informal, conversational, open-ended interviews to collect data regarding the lived experience of honor among first generation Levantine Arab American women. The interviewing approach to be used for this study was the informal, conversational interview (Moustakas, 1990, p. 47) which involves the researcher asking the co-researcher the interview questions while still allowing for spontaneous questions to come up during the interview. The primary researcher interviewed one co-researcher at a time, at a rate of one to two co-researchers per month. Each co-researcher was interviewed one time. It is important that the conversation be as natural as possible so that the co-researcher felt comfortable giving over this sensitive information about their personal lives. Each co-researcher was asked a series of questions regarding their lived experience of honor. The first question asked during the open- ended interviews was "what is your lived experience of honor?" The co-researcher was given as much time as they need to answer in full. The interviews were digitally recorded and the researcher intervened during the answering process as little as possible to ensure the data collected was as pure, uninterrupted, and as unbiased as it could be.

As part of the heuristic process, the researcher collected her own data by answering the research question and the interview questions in a journal. The researcher journaled about her own lived experience of honor. In addition to answering the interview questions, the researcher continued the journaling process during the entire data collection and data analysis process. The researcher documented her experiences, her reactions to the data collected, to the connections found between her experience and the co-researchers. After each interview, the researcher would jot down field notes, later transcribe them into the laptop. This is the same password protected laptop used to record the interviews. Following each interview, the researcher provided each co-researcher a journal, which contained a copy of the interview questions. In this journal, co-researchers were kindly asked for their written answers to the guiding research questions, as they may differ from (or they may add to) what was brought up during the interviews. A prepaid, addressed envelope was provided with the journal so that the co-researcher may mail it back to the researcher with minimal imposition. The researcher requested that the journals be sent back within four weeks of the interview. The co-researcher may choose not to participate in the journaling. Of the 13 participants whose data was utilized in this study, 10 participants sent back completed journals to the researcher. Once all the data

was documented, and transcribed, the researcher began the analysis of the data (audio and

journals).

Data Analysis

The researcher remained consistent in regards to data analysis in heuristic

methodology, as it was developed and outlined by Moustakas (1990).

1. The researcher gathered data and organized it accordingly for each co-researcher.

2. The researcher immersed herself in the collected data. The researcher would re-read, re-listen to the interview transcripts and audio. The researcher also reviewed the journalings of the co-researchers. This review repeatedly occurred until the researcher was satisfied that the co-researcher's experience was clear and understood.

3. Following the intense period of immersion, the researcher also took time away from the material. This meant taking the time to step away from each interview, to attempt to gain a fresh perspective and revitalize the researcher in regards to the material. Once rested in regards to the material, the researcher returned to it once more. At this point, the primary researcher reviewed all the co-researcher's data for any relevant themes and patterns. The primary researcher took notes regarding the data that most clearly emphasized the individual's depiction of the experience, all the while maintaining the co-searcher's story and language used to express it.

4. At this point in the journey, after taking time away from the material, the researcher returned to the data of each co-researcher. The primary researcher reviewed each interview and journal. In the process of reviewing each co-researcher's data, the primary researcher verified the data collected, and the experience conveyed. This process is referred to as "member checking" and is a way to establish credibility in qualitative research (McBrien, 2008). This overview of the individual depiction of the experience and verification was repeated for each co-researcher.

5. Once one co-researcher's depiction of the experience had been completed, the primary researcher uses the same process as defined in step four to complete an accurate depiction of the experience for the remainder of the co-researchers.

6. Now that the researcher has gone through each interview, each journal, and identified the emergent themes and patterns, she was now able to draw a collective image of the experience. The primary researcher now engaged in the immersion process. In this immersion process the researcher while taking breaks from the data, compiles a composite collected. In this composite collective, the researcher used the co-researchers' narrative, the language, and the verbatim words captured in interviews. These pieces are the paint with which the researcher creates a vivid and illustrative picture of the whole lived experience. A composite collective is achieved when "all of the core meanings of the phenomenon as experienced by the individual participants and by the group as a whole" (Moustakas, 1990, p. 52).

7. Lastly, the researcher went through each interview and journal of each co-researcher. The primary researcher looks for the few cases that best exemplified the group as a whole. The primary researcher chose three co-researchers, the researcher spotlighted each co-researcher's experience, by utilizing their data and their depictions of the experience, to create an individual portrait of the experience.

8. In the final step of the creative synthesis, the researcher has now developed a vivid and illustrative description of the experience being studied. "The researcher as a scientist-artist develops an aesthetic rendition of the themes and essential meanings of the phenomenon" (Moustakas, 1990, p. 52). In this final rendition, the knowledge the primary researcher has collected through the processes of heuristic inquiry are reflected and illustrated. Illustrated as the primary researcher's knowledge of and passion regarding the material having manifested itself in the form of "narrative, story, poem, work of art, metaphor, analogy or tale" (Moustakas, 1990, p. 52). Each step of the data analysis process has allowed the primary researcher to (in a cyclical way) obtain the data, explore the data, verify the data through constant review, and depict the experience in the most illustrative way possible utilizing the co-researcher's direct quotes.

Credibility

In qualitative research, to be credible is to be valid (Hoepfl, 1997). Therefore, to achieve credibility in heuristic research, it is imperative to utilize direct quotes from the co-researchers. In addition, the co-researchers must trust the primary researcher. Douglas and Moustakas (1985) add that increased credibility comes when the co-researchers express the same experience. Specifically, heuristic research "is inherent, insofar as it pursues the truth, to the extent that it is conducted through authentic self-processes, and to the degree that after repeated examinations of the data, the same essences are revealed with the same degree of plausibility" (p. 44). The primary researcher was constantly engaging the co-researchers in dialogue to ensure that the experiences were being expressed clearly and accurately. Finally, the primary researcher practiced the detailed steps of the heuristic method. By becoming fluent in the heuristic methodology, the primary researcher increased the credibility of the study.

The primary researcher utilized Moustakas' (1990) idea of checking and rechecking the data, "the heuristic researcher returns again and again to the data to check the depictions of the experience to determine whether the qualities or constituents that have been derived from the data embrace the necessary and sufficient meanings" (p. 24). The techniques utilized in heuristic inquiry allowed the primary researcher to not only enable the gathering of quality data from the participants but also allow for the best application of the methodology by the primary researcher. It is the step-by-step process of Heuristic Inquiry that kept the study credible as the primary researcher followed each step (Initial Engagement, Immersion, Incubation, Illumination, Explication, Creative Synthesis). By applying each step of Heuristic Inquiry to the data collected, the primary researcher ensured the study remained credible. In addition, the constant checking and referencing back to the data ensured the validity and credibility of the study. The rechecking helped "enable the researcher to achieve repeated verification that the explication of the phenomenon and the creative synthesis of essences and meanings actually portray the phenomenon investigated (Moustakas, 1990, p. 30).

In regards to transferability, Patton (1990) described a study that has transferability as one that has "gone beyond the narrow confines of the data to think about other applications of the findings" (p. 489). The study represented the targeted population by utilizing the experiences of the sample population. By utilizing Arab American women between the ages of 25-35, who are from the Levant (Lebanon, Syria, Jordan, Egypt, Palestinian territories, and Israel), the primary researcher found that the findings of the study are transferable and relatable to the population at large of Arab American Levantine women.

In regards to dependability, the researcher followed Moustakas' (1990) steps of heuristic inquiry, in detail. The researcher followed the steps of research (Initial Engagement, Immersion, Incubation, Illumination, Explication, Creative Synthesis) and gave a detailed, vivid description of the methodology of the study. This will allow other researchers to complete the study in the same manner, utilizing the same methods, and replicate the same findings. In addition, the researcher was vigilant in her data collection, interpretation of data, and the reporting of the data. The heuristic protocol was followed with each participant, each interview, and each bit of data.

Target Population and Participant Selection

Sample Size

The projected sample size of the study was 8-14 participants or until data saturation was achieved. Data saturation occurs when the researcher no longer hears or sees any new information regarding the experience. Polkinghorne (2005) explained that qualitative studies focus on the understanding and explaining of a specific experience. For this to happen, the study needs to collect descriptions of that experience that are saturated. When this occurs, the researcher does not need to collect additional data.

The total number of co-researchers in this study was 13 individuals, including the researcher. Moustakas (1990) suggests keeping the sample size small to study the lived experience in depth. The smaller sample size may reduce the study's generalizability. However it allows for a specific exploration of a lived experience, the lived experience of honor. The consistency of the experience across the interviews of the co-researchers increased the study's credibility.

Procedures

Sampling Procedures

The researcher utilized the intensity sampling strategy. Described by Patton (1990) as "consisting of information rich cases that manifest the phenomenon of interest intensely (but not extremely)" (p. 234). In total, the researcher obtained data from 13 co-researchers. As the researcher in this Heuristic study, the researcher participated as one of the cases that manifest the phenomenon of the lived experience on honor. There was an intense interest and experience in regards to the research question, on behalf of the researcher. There was an intense experience in regards to the co-researchers studied; therefore, the requirements of both Heuristic inquiry and intensity sampling were met. Patton (1990) also mentioned, "Intensity sampling involves some prior information and considerable judgment" (p. 234). The researcher has prior experience regarding the phenomenon of lived experience of honor in first generation Levantine Arab American women, as she is part of that group.

Recruitment

The co-researchers were recruited through flyers posted in businesses around a

Muslim Community Center and Mosque in an urban metro area in the North East. The

flyer included the researcher's contact information as well as the basic information about

the study; the type of co-researcher requested, what is the topic of interest, and the extent

of time needed from the co-researcher. After the co-researchers had been screened to

meet the inclusion criteria (whether they are appropriate to participate in the study;

specifically age, specify whether they are first generation American, Levantine country of

origin, and interest in the phenomenon), appointments were set up for interviews.

Participants were emailed a copy of the consent form for their review before the

interview (stating the purpose of the study, amount of time needed from each co-

researcher, verification of the co-researcher's interest in the research question, and

verification of the co-researcher's consent to participate in the study).

A meeting time with the co-researcher was arranged, at their convenience. The

researcher inquired about the reservation of a private room of a local library in which to

conduct the interviews. The room included the researcher's laptop for recording, the

researcher's notebook for field notes, the informed consent form, and water for the co-

researcher. The researcher waited for the co-researcher at the door of the room, after

giving detailed directions as how to find them. Once co-researcher made their way to the

room, the researcher was able to greet them. In this greeting, the researcher introduced

themselves and gave the co-researcher a moment to ask any questions the co-researcher

might have. The researcher described the nature of the study and provided a consent form to the co-researcher, the consent form is to be signed. Once the consent form was signed, the recorded informal, conversational interviews began.

Each co-researcher was given a $10 Starbucks gift card upon completion of the interview. Co-researchers were also given the researcher's contact information, as well as a list of mental health service locations to be used if needed.

Protection of Participants

There were concerns about the privacy of the co-researchers. The researcher acquired a separate cell phone line that is password protected for the potential co-researchers to call or make contact with the researcher. All interviews were conducted in a private, sound proof room at a local college library (reserved by the researcher). Participants were informed that each interview would be digitally recorded and stored on a password-protected laptop. The journal with the researcher's data is kept in a password-protected file on the researcher's computer (for seven years, after which the data will be destroyed) which is also password-protected. The co-researchers were identified by number only, (for example, Co-researcher 1, Co-researcher 2, etc.). All identifying formation is disregarded. The co-researchers were informed that there was no penalty for withdrawing from the study at any time, should they feel the need to do so. If they chose to remove themselves from the study, the researcher would surrender any data affiliated with that co-researcher. No co-researchers withdrew from the study at any point. After all the interviews had been conducted, the researcher sent the recordings to a transcribing service. The transcriber hired signed a confidentiality agreement before accessing the data for transcription.

Data Collection

After the primary researcher has established initial contact during recruitment and had cleared the co-researchers for participation, the primary researcher organized a meeting time for the interview to be conducted. The primary researcher greeted the potential participant at the door of the local library and escorted them into the reserved room. Utilizing informal, conversational, open-ended interviews to collect data, the primary researcher was able to collect data regarding the lived experience of honor among first generation Levantine Arab American women. During the interview, the co-researcher was asked a series of guiding questions regarding their lived experience of honor. The opening question asked during the open- ended interviews was "what is your lived experience of honor?" The co-researchers were given as much time as they needed to answer in full, with minimal intervention from the primary researcher. The interviews were digitally recorded; this ensured the data collected was as pure, uninterrupted, and as unbiased as it could be.

As part of the heuristic process, the primary researcher collected her answers to the guiding questions by answering the interview questions digitally as well as in a journal. The primary researcher also continued the journaling process during the entire data collection and data analysis process. The primary researcher documented her experiences, her reactions to the data collected, to the connections found between her experience and the co-researchers. After each interview, the primary researcher took the time to take down field notes, afterward, would transcribe them into her laptop. The laptop is the same password protected laptop used to record the interviews and store the data collected. After the interview had been completed, the primary researcher provided each co-researcher a journal, which contained a copy of the interview questions. In the provided journal, co-researchers were asked for their written responses to the guiding interview research questions, if they were to differ from (or they add to) the responses in the interviews. Each co-researcher was given a prepaid, addressed envelope with the journal so that the co-researcher may mail it back to the researcher with minimal imposition. The researcher requested that the journals be returned within four weeks of the interview, to give the primary researcher ample time to evaluate the journal responses. The co-researcher may choose not to participate in the journaling. Of the 13 participants whose data was utilized in this study, 10 participants sent back completed journals to the researcher. Once all the data was documented, and transcribed, the researcher began the analysis of the data (audio and journals). Upon receiving IRB approval, the researcher began data collection.

Data Analysis

Moustakas (1990) outlined the eight steps of data analysis that were used for the data collected in this study. First, the primary researcher was to gather all the data. Second, the primary researcher was to enter immersion into the data until it was fully understood. Third, set the data aside to have a fresh perspective once the primary researcher returned to the data. Fourth, after a period of rest, the primary researcher returned to the data. Fifth, the primary researcher gathered the individual experiences together in a group to represent the experience as a whole. Sixth, again the primary researcher immersed themselves in the data. Seventh, the primary researcher chose three co-researcher's experiences that best illustrated the experience. In the eighth and final step, the primary researcher utilized creative synthesis to develop a clear and illustrative picture of the co-researchers' experience of honor among first generation Levantine Arab American women.

Analysis of the data collected was used to develop the individual depictions of each co-researcher's experience. This analysis involved extended immersion into the data collected until the primary researcher was fully acquainted with the data. The journals returned by the co-researchers were synthesized and utilized data essential to the study. However, the process of synthesis, the data collected took on a narrative form, using direct quotes and examples. Once the data had been analyzed, the primary researcher returned to the transcriptions to ensure the authenticity and accuracy of the depictions of the experience.

Data Presentation

The findings of the study are presented in *Chapter 4: Data Collection and Analysis*. The findings are presented in a manner that is consistent with the heuristic methodology. Following the description of each participant and the description of the sample as a whole, the key themes of each participant's experience are presented sequentially, followed by illustrative quotes regarding the themes, which allow the experience to be illuminated. The emergent themes were analyzed and presented to each participant. Following the presentation of the emergent themes in the data, the researcher generated emergent patterns in the data. Illustrative quotes regarding the patterns were utilized to present a clear understanding of each pattern presented. The emergent patterns were analyzed and presented for each participant.

Following the presentation of the emergent themes and patterns for each participant, the researcher presented a composite collective. In this composite, the researcher used the participant's narrative, the language, and the verbatim words captured in interviews. In addition, the researcher presented a few cases that best exemplified the lived experience of honor as a whole. The researcher chose three participants and showcased each participant's experience, interview, and journal. The researcher utilized direct quotes from the participant's interviews and journals to illustrate further the experience.

Researcher's Bias

The primary researcher has identified possible biases and has laid out a plan to reduce them. The first possible bias the primary researcher may have is the assumption that all first generation, Levantine, Arab American women have similar experiences of honor across various aspects of their lives, whether it is personally or professionally. As the researcher has lived with honor having an impact on her daily life, she may assume that the participants also lived with honor affecting their daily lives. The researcher understood that this might not have been the experience of honor for all the participants in the study. The researcher's experience was used to inform the research question, provide sensitivity and understanding during the interview process, and give the study an additional resource in regards to data.

Previous knowledge of the experience had to be set aside to gain a fresh perspective on the phenomenon being studied. To gain this fresh perspective, the primary researcher chose to collect her own data before the data of the co-researchers. By fully expressing her experience of honor, the researcher was able to acknowledge and recognize her own experience and put it aside before starting to collect the data of the co-researchers. The primary researcher was able to remain objective to the experiences of the co-researchers while practicing self-awareness and self-reflexivity during the data collection process.

Instruments

Guiding Questions

In heuristic inquiry, the primary researcher becomes the instrument of research. The researcher developed a series of guiding questions. These questions allowed the researcher to cover all areas of interest regarding the topic of the study. The questions also allowed the researcher to guide the interview process to ensure the most information was obtained. The following questions guided the interview process:

1. How would you describe your life experience of honor?

2. What was your earliest memory in regards to honor in your life? How did it make you feel?

3. What aspects or qualities of honor are important to you? Why do you think they are important to you?

4. How does the lived experience of honor influence your view of the world and your place in it?

5. What does honor mean to you today? How does that make you feel?

6. Is there anything I have not asked you that you would like to share about the lived experience of honor?

Role of the Researcher

The primary researcher was the author of the guiding interview questions and the interviewer in this study. This dual role is unique and essential to heuristic inquiry. The primary researcher is essentially an instrument of data collection and later, analysis. In taking on this role, the primary researcher set aside her own bias and preconceived notions. The primary researcher acknowledges the issues of bias regarding the

68

assumption of the co-researchers' lives being impacted by honor and the suspension of

that assumption, collected her data first in order to suspend her own experience later

when collecting co-researcher's data. In addition, the primary researcher consistently

used self-awareness and self-reflexivity during the data collection, presentation, and

analysis processes.

In regards to analysis of the data that has been collected, the researcher is the

instrument used to analyze the data. Moustakas (1990) stated that there is an "emphasis

on the investigator's internal frame of reference, self-searching, intuition, and indwelling

lies at the heart of heuristic research" (p. 12). The researcher was the instrument used to

analyze the experience because the researcher has also experienced the phenomenon

being studied. As the study is being conducted, the researcher was present and developed

a deeper understanding of the phenomenon. With that growth of understanding, the

researcher became more self-aware and self-understanding of their lived experience. The

researcher's role is not limited to data collection. The researcher is to understand their

experience of the phenomenon, acknowledging their experience during the analysis. This

simultaneous analysis and understanding of the researcher and co-researcher experience

is why Moustakas (1990) refers to the co-researchers as co-researchers.

In regards to experience and training in utilizing Moustakas' Heuristic Inquiry

and interviewing, this was the researcher's first time implementing this particular

methodology. However, the researcher has completed a series of research courses at

Capella University including; Research Methods, Qualitative Analysis, Advanced

Qualitative Analysis, and Quantitative Research Methods. The researcher has also

completed her Master's thesis utilizing phenomenology as the research methodology. The researcher has developed her listening and assessment skills in her work as an adjunct

college professor in Religious Studies.

Research Questions and Hypotheses

The research question for this study is "What is the lived experience of honor

among Levantine Arab American Women?" In contrast to the design of quantitative

research, which aims to either prove or disprove a hypothesis, qualitative research looks

to illuminate an experience. This leaves the research open to a variety of outcomes, as

opposed to a set outcome. Due to the nature of qualitative research, this study did not

require a hypothesis, rather the study allowed the co-researcher's experience to speak to

and illustrate the phenomenon.

Data Analysis

Continuing to follow the heuristic procedure and methods for data analysis laid

out by Moustakas (1990), the primary researcher took the following steps during data

analysis:

1. The primary researcher gathered all data from one participant at a time
   (interview, journal, and interview transcript) to organize and analyze at a time.

2. The primary researcher immersed herself in the collected data until it was
   completely understood and the co-researcher's experience was understood in
   detail. The primary researcher completed this step with each of the co-
   researcher's collected data.

3. The collected data was set aside by the primary researcher for a period to
   allow the primary researcher a rest from the information. The primary
   researcher then could return to the collected data with a fresh perspective.
   This period of rest occurred several times during the data collection process,
   allowing the primary researcher to develop a clear depiction of the experience
   of the co-researcher. Once the individual depiction of the experience for each
   co-researcher is developed, the primary researcher returned to the original
   data (one co-researcher at a time) to make sure the experience depicted fit the

data collected. During this period, the primary researcher was looking for emergent themes and patterns relevant to the experience being explored by the study. Once the primary researcher was satisfied that the data has been correctly analyzed, checked against the data, searched for emergent themes or patterns, she would then move on to repeat this process with the data collected of the next co-researcher.

4. Throughout the process of data analysis, the primary researcher experienced periods of insight and breakthroughs regarding the emergent themes and patterns in the data collected. In this step of data analysis, the primary researcher returned to the data collected from each co-researcher separately. The primary researcher shared the data collected with the co-researcher and verified two things; "does the individual depiction of the experience fit the data from which it was developed? Does it contain the qualities and themes essential to the experience?" (Moustakas, 1990, p. 51). The co-researchers were able to verify the data was accurate, allowing the primary researcher and moved on to analyze the next co-researcher's data.

5. Each of the above steps, step one through step four was repeated for each co-researcher. The primary researcher constantly verified the data for each co-researcher, ensuring that the experience was authentic in collection, depiction and presentation. After going through each co-researcher's data, the researcher was able to develop an illustrated experience for each co-researcher based on the data collected.

6. Once primary researcher had completed all the data analysis for all the co-researchers, a composite group depiction was developed which illustrated the emergent themes and patterns that depicted the experience overall. Through periods of intense internal reflection and referencing back to her own frame of reference, the primary researcher was able to develop an illustrative and inclusive depiction of the experience of honor among first generation, Levantine, Arab American women.

7. The primary researcher reviewed each of the co-researcher's data and in doing so, looked for three cases that exemplified the experience best. These portraits illustrated the experience of the co-researchers by explaining in detail, using direct quotes, the experience being studied.

8. In the process of developing of a creative synthesis of the experience, the primary researcher was able to utilize the data collected from the co-researchers, her own experience, and the knowledge developed during the periods of immersion, illumination, and explication of the experience. "The researcher as a scientist-artist develops an aesthetic rendition of the themes and essential meanings of the phenomenon" (Moustakas, 1990, p. 52). This last stage of data analysis is characterized by a final rendition of the experience being studied.

Heuristics allows the researcher to not only explore a phenomenon as it occurs, but also to share their experience of the phenomenon. There are any number of ways creative synthesis can take form; poetic narrative, storytelling, through art, through song, or analogy (Moustakas, 1990, p. 52). Heuristic inquiry allows the researcher and co-researchers to utilize creative synthesis in whatever mode they feel best to convey their experience. The researcher finalized the emergent themes and patterns of all the co-researchers into a composite depiction that illustrated the lived experience of first generation, Levantine, Arab American women. The researcher utilized exemplary quotes, from the co-researcher's interviews, that provided vivid support for the themes and patterns in the composite depiction.

In regards to the storage and protection of the collected data, all the recorded and transcribed interviews were stored on a password-protected laptop computer. All of the co-researcher's names were changed (Co-researcher 1, Co-researcher 2, etc.) and any identifying information was removed. The primary researcher recorded the interviews and sent the recordings to be transcribed by a service, where the transcriber signed a confidentiality agreement. The primary researcher alone has access to the laptop; the password is only known to the researcher. All of the data will be erased from the primary researcher's laptop after seven years.

Ethical Considerations

Before the co-researchers were recruited for the study, the researcher completed the IRB application. When working with human subjects, the IRB has published a report that addresses the concerns and rights of the participants. The Belmont Report outlines the responsibility of the researcher, specifically regarding issues of beneficence, justice, and respect of the person (The National Institutes of Health, 1979). The researcher's IRB Application was reviewed by the IRB and approved before any data was collected by the researcher.

In regards to beneficence (National Institutes of Health, 1979, p. 15), the researcher is ordered to do no harm. In line with this order, the researcher has provided an informed consent form. This allowed the co-researcher to understand the purpose of the study, the requirements to participate, and a listing of the risks and benefits if they co-researcher chooses to participate. All the co-researcher's questions were answered and they were given time to consider their participation. The co-researchers were told explicitly during the recruitment phase that there was the option to withdraw at any time, should they choose to do so. The study did not include a vulnerable population therefore, it met the requirements for a study with minimal risk.

Expected Findings

In accordance with the heuristic process, this study was a process of discovery and illumination on the lived experience of honor. As such, there were no expected findings. Rather, the researcher approached the heuristic process with the intent to uncover a phenomenon. The intent of the study was to first, uncover the experience through the data collected from the co-researchers. Second, highlight the shared experiences of the co-researchers and the researcher regarding the phenomenon. Because this researcher is also a Levantine Arab American woman, her experiences were a part of the study. It was the expectation of the researcher that the heuristic process would lead to an understanding of the lived experience of honor among Levantine Arab American women. Although the primary researcher had an idea that her co-researchers would have some experiences regarding honor, she did not have any assumptions or preconceived

notions of the study's outcome.

CHAPTER 4. DATA COLLECTION AND ANALYSIS

Introduction: The Study and the Researcher

This chapter focuses on presenting the findings of the research question: "What is the lived experience of honor among first generation Levantine Arab American women?" In this chapter, there is a presentation of data collection process as well as the use of Moustakas' (1990) heuristic methodology in the data analysis. The research question was brought to light by the primary researcher's own experience with the phenomenon as well as the co-researcher's shared experience.

The chapter is divided into four parts, beginning with the primary researcher's background and interest or motivation to research this experience. Second, there is a description of the co-researcher's demographics. Third, there is a discussion of the heuristic methodology as it is applied to the data analysis. There will then be a presentation of the data collected including the researcher's journal entries, developed patterns and themes. There will also be illustrative portraits of the lived experience.

The primary researcher has always had a strong interest in the experience of honor and an intense desire to study the experience. The primary researcher is a first generation Levantine Arab American woman, and being so had the intense experience of honor throughout her childhood and adult life. Having spoken to other first generation Levantine Arab American women throughout her life, she found that the experience of honor was not one that was exclusive to her, but rather a shared experience. Given the primary researcher's background, her motivation to conduct this study was both professional and personal. Professional in that there was a serious need to study the experience of honor in the United States as there is an increase in Arab immigration to the United States (D'Agostino, 2002). Personal, in that there was a desire to uncover and understand an experience that was central to her understanding of herself and her culture. In addition, the primary researcher's main goal was to use the heuristic process to represent the experience of first generation Levantine Arab American women, who as of yet have not been represented in the literature regarding the experience of honor.

The primary researcher has not used heuristic inquiry before this study however, has used phenomenology in her Master's thesis during her graduate work at Columbia University. In addition, the primary researcher has completed a series of research courses at her time at Capella University including; Research Methods, Qualitative Analysis, Advanced Qualitative Analysis, and Quantitative Research Methods. In addition, the researcher has attended all three colloquia tracks and has completed relevant research coursework within those tracks. The primary researcher collected data from the co-researchers and from herself. During the data collection process, the primary researcher kept a journal to illustrate her experience of honor further and more in depth. As the primary researcher had similar or shared experiences of honor as some of the co-researchers, she was sensitive to the effects she may have on the co-researchers and the data collected. To avoid this, the primary researcher made sure not to allow her own experience or biases to effect the co-researchers during interview or the data collected.

Description of the Sample (Participants)

Thirteen co-researchers, which included the primary researcher, participated in this study. The co-researchers ages ranged from 25 to 35. All of the participants were first generation, Levantine Arab American women and US citizens. All thirteen of the co-researchers and the primary researcher lived in the tri-state area of New York, New Jersey, and Connecticut. Of the 13 co-researchers and the primary researcher; three were married, ten were single, two had children, and all 13 were employed. Six of the co-researchers were Muslim, five were Christian, and two were non-religious. The co-researchers represented the Levant in the Middle East, which includes Lebanon, Syria, Jordan, Egypt, Palestinian territories, and Israel. Two co-researchers had one child each at the time of interview. Each of the 13 co-researchers was enthusiastic to participate in the study. During the interview process, the co-researchers gave much insight to the experience and were very informative. None of the co-researchers who participated in the study dropped out at any time.

Research Methodology Applied to the Data Analysis

The primary researcher had applied Moustakas' (1990) heuristic research methodology to the data in regards to analysis. The following eight steps were used in analyzing the data collected by the primary researcher:

1. The data from one co-researcher was gathered, organized and synthesized. The data from this co-researcher included the transcribed interview, journal notes from the co-researcher and any field notes from the primary researcher.

2. The primary researcher had then immersed herself in all the data collected for the first co-researcher.

3. After this period of immersion, the primary researcher set the data aside, allowing for a rest from the material. Following this break, the co-researcher

77

went through the data once more to look for any emergent themes and patterns.

4. Once the themes and patterns were identified, the researcher reviewed the co-researcher's original data to make sure the revealed experience was accurate in regards to the experience depicted in the data. The primary researcher shared the depiction revealed with the co-researcher to affirm the depiction was correct. All co-researchers confirmed the experience was accurate.

5. As the first co-researcher's data was completed in regards to analysis and depiction, the primary researcher was free to move on to the following co-researcher's data until each set of data for each co-researcher was completed.

6. Following the complete analysis of all the co-researcher's data, the primary researcher was then able to immerse herself into the data of all the co-researchers as a whole. This period of immersion included a period of time where the primary researcher took time away from the data. During the period of immersion, the primary researcher was able to develop a composite depiction of the experience, as it was experienced by the primary researcher and the co-researchers.

7. After reviewing the data in regards to the experiences rendered, the primary researcher chose three co-researchers whose experience most clearly represented and illustrated the experience being studied. Each co-researcher had an illustrative portrait of their experience developed using their transcribed interviews, journal notes, and the primary researcher's field notes.

8. Finally, the composite experience of the phenomenon being studied was presented in a narrative form. Utilizing the data collected from herself and the co-researcher's, the primary researcher was able to create a clear and illustrative depiction of the experience using the themes and patterns discovered. There were no differences from the data analysis protocol outlined in chapter three. The primary researcher did not come upon any issues with data collection or data analysis.

Presentation of the Data and Results of the Analysis

After an extensive amount of time in the investigative phases of research, followed by the processes of immersion and incubation, 22 patterns emerged from the collected data that solidified the lived experience of honor among first generation Levantine Arab American women, ages 25-35. The patterns observed are as follows:

- Forbidding Sex/Forbidding socializing with boys

- Education

- Honor resides in the Female body

- Importance of a "Good Marriage"

- Importance of Virginity

- Family rules

- Community rules

- Respect for your family

- Self-respect

- Inappropriate relationships

- Feelings of Shame

- Feelings of fear

- Guilt

- Modesty

- Being judged

- Being ostracized

- Trust between parent and child

- Disappointing your parent

- Independence

- Parents

- Lack of communication between parent and child

- Being a "Good girl"

After the primary researcher established the patterns, the primary researcher

utilized Moustakas' (1990) data analysis procedure to identify the themes in regards to the patterns discovered: virginity, social status, parental role, shame, and relationships with children/future children.

The patterns that demonstrate each theme are organized into themes as follows:

- Theme 1: Virginity
    - Pattern 1.1: Honor resides in the Female body
    - Pattern 1.2: Self-respect
    - Pattern 1.3: Being a "good girl"
    - Pattern: 1.4: Modesty

- Theme 2: Social Status
    - Pattern 2.1: Being judged
    - Pattern 2.2 Being ostracized
    - Pattern 2.3: Education
    - Pattern 2.4: Importance of a "Good Marriage"

- Theme 3: Parental Role
    - Pattern 3.1: Lack of Communication between parent and child
    - Pattern 3.2: Forbidding Socializing with boys /Forbidding sex
    - Pattern 3.3: Family Rules
    - Pattern 3.4 Guilt

- Theme 4: Shame
    - Pattern 4.1: Disappointing your parents
    - Pattern 4.2: Inappropriate Relationships
    - Pattern 4.3: Community Rules
    - Pattern 4.4: Importance of virginity

- Theme 5: Looking Ahead

- o Pattern 5.1 Trust between parent and child

- o Pattern 5.2 Independence

- o Pattern 5.3 Respect for your family

- o Pattern 5.4 Relationships with Children/Future Children

The Primary Researcher's Data

As the primary researcher is a participant in her own study, the guiding interview questions were also answered and analyzed. In the following journal entries, the primary researcher reflected on her experience. Utilizing memories and her own feelings, the primary researcher was able to answer the question: What is the lived experience of honor among first generation Levantine Arab American women? The journal entries are organized in order of appearance.

Journal Entry 1

> I come from a mixed home, Arab and American, my father did assimilate into American culture to a point. He has a successful business, a large home, etc. However, his children, especially his female children, were to behave honorably. The girls had to be "good" girls. So, growing up I didn't do what other girls normally did. For example, no sleepovers. You never know who would be there, if the girlfriend had brothers or a parent who may behave inappropriately. Looking back now, at my age and I have kids, I totally am on board with that. I hear about children getting molested at friend's houses all the time and are scarred for life. However, on the other side of the argument, dating was an issue. We were in our teens and we weren't "allowed" to date. Which is absurd in American culture, in high school! Everyone else was going to movies, getting asked to dances. We couldn't go with dates, with boys. Because we were girls. Our brothers didn't have the same set of rules. If we were to do something like that, we were being dishonorable, *eib,* fresh. No one would want to marry a girl who was considered dirty, used, damaged. And the way you get to be any of those things was to do unsupervised, unapproved things, or outings with boys or men.

Journal Entry 2

> I remember being picked up at school in grade school. My father always wore a black leather jacket and ran up to a man, who I thought was my father in that type

of jacket and I jumped on his back. He turned around and it wasn't my father. I
was quickly placed on the ground by the gentleman and heard my dad yelling for
me across the parking lot. I got yelled at several times about not jumping on men
and it was *eib,* fresh and not appropriate behavior. I explained to my father that I
had mistaken that man for him and he firmly told me I shouldn't even be jumping
on him. I am a big girl now and my behavior has to be that of a lady. I was 9. I
felt embarrassed and upset that I had visibly disappointed my father. I think back
on it now that maybe it wasn't disappointment on his face I was reading, but
maybe sadness. I was growing up and there were a new set of dangers before me.
The dangers of sex and pregnancy. The dangers of a tarnished reputation. The
dangers of not having marriage prospects because of my behavior. At that point
on, I was constantly made aware of these dangers and the effects they would have
on my life, my future. Focus on school. Education, education, education was my
father's mantra.

Journal Entry 3

I think that conservative sexual practices are an important aspect of honor. Girls
and boys, but mostly girls should be careful and not as free with their bodies.
Girls more so because we bear the brunt of the sexual encounter. Pregnancy,
social stigma, etc. The physical component of honor is the most important one I
think. It is the one that's most important for women, anyway. Maintaining "clean"
image or reputation is important to me and I think most Arab women because it
directly affects your social standing, which directly affects your marriage
prospects which directly affects your family. This cycle was drilled into my head
all through my adolescence. I am not just acting for myself in my actions, I am
acting for my family. My actions don't just affect me, they affect my family.
Honor was important to my family so therefore honor was important to me.

Journal Entry 4

Honor means not putting yourself in any position that could cause you or your
family any type of harm. Physical, emotional, social harm. So all aspects of my
behavior directly affects my family so if I love my family I would take great care
not to do anything that would put them in any type of harm's way. I have done
things that normal teenagers did, and I remember the embarrassment on my
father's face, the gossiping of other Arab people in our community. I never want
to do that to him again. It makes me feel physically sick when I think of how I
have disappointed and embarrassed my parents with my dishonorable behavior.

Journal Entry 5

I read an article in the newspaper today, a young girl who had been gunned down
by a younger brother because she had been caught dating and dishonored her

family. This happened here in the US. It is just so unreal to me that this could happen. That a father and a mother could not only let it happen but give the son permission and encouragement to do so. How could the brother do it? I can't wrap my mind around it. And I realize that the community is responsible. If there wasn't such a high premium placed on virginity, it wouldn't be an issue. If there wasn't such a social stigma about it, it wouldn't be an issue. If people would not be treated like pariahs, this wouldn't be an issue. It's a social practice that is upheld by the whole community but it shouldn't. We are hurting ourselves and we are hurting our daughters.

Journal Entry 6

I know that most people think of the worst when they think of Arabs or Islam. That we are a culture of people who kill their daughters for dating and hate all Americans. But we love America. We love being in a country that allows us to practice our faith freely. There are some Arabs who are slower to assimilate and maybe come from cultures that do condone violence towards women who behave dishonorably. But that's not the majority. With that said, I think it's important to note that the conservative culture of Arab people is one I grew up with, had issues with, but will still raise my children in. I want to protect my children from the dangers of the world. Aside from informing them of what's out there, I want to protect them with my rules and regulations.

Journal Entry 7

Is it a big deal to have multiple boyfriends? It is when you grow up but I think as a child, if you have one boyfriend a year, 6th grade, 7th grade, it's not that big of a deal. I mean I understand serial monogamy. There is an extent to that but with our family, to my father, there was no extent. It was just nobody. You don't want to hear about it, you don't want to see nothing; nothing had to be happening kind of thing. If he found out, he would have been very, very, very unhappy and I would know it.

Journal Entry 8

I remember my older cousin was talking to a boy in our neighborhood. She was sneaking around seeing him. Secret phone calls. Notes at school. I was 8 or 9. I remember feeling a lot of anxiety and fear. Nervous for her if her father or her brother saw what she was doing. At that age, I was already being lectured about boys. They only want one thing, etc. So, if I was nervous for her I can't imagine how nervous and scared she must have been to get caught. She never got caught but all the girl cousins knew about her and her running around.

Journal Entry 9

In the news, we see these horrible stories. These fathers killing daughters for dishonoring the family. Talking to boys etc. I would like to say "no, that only happens in third world countries, it's not happening here" But it is. There are immigrant families who come here, bring their values with them. They are immersed in the American culture, there is no slow transition. You come here and that's it. No time to get used to it. I had all my life to get used to it. To make my own judgments and choices of the American life. But my parents had a lot of issues getting used to what was acceptable. And maybe they were harder on us in regards to honor and our behavior because they were so shocked as to what was appropriate here. I think that there is definitely a push back on the side of the parents. Push back against full on acceptance of "American" culture and action.

Journal Entry 10

Different aspects of honor that are important to me are the honor I have for myself. I believe that for me to honor myself I have to be proud of who I am as a person, which helps me thrive to be a good person with high moral values. The honor and respect people have for me- I believe that I, regardless of my beliefs, whether they are different than the people in my surroundings or not I deserve to be respected. And I shouldn't be judged because of my religious views or the culture I was born into. Honor I have for the people around me- I strongly believe that we should treat people the way we want to be treated. I believe that no matter what religion or culture people around me are from we should all respect each other regardless of our differences. This is very important to me because my respect and value for others reflects on myself.

Patterns and Themes

The patterns discovered were organized into themes to assist in the illustration of

the lived experience of honor among first generation Levantine Arab American women.

Each theme is described and after the description will be verbatim quotes from the data

that will support the theme being discussed.

Theme 1: Virginity

The lived experience of honor among first generation Levantine Arab American

women begins with the importance of virginity. Virginity did not seem limited to the

84

hymen remaining intact until marriage. It also seemed to include a perception of the female and her behavior. While the physical virginity was most important, the perception of the female was also critical. It is critical that the female behaves accordingly and not bring her physical virginity into question. There is an intense desire to preserve the female and her virginity in every way possible. There is a fear that freedom means loss of virginity.

Pattern1.1 Honor resides in the female body. Many of the co-researchers described virginity as being something they physically had. The hymen remaining intact is a physical sign of virginity; the hymen seems to be where the honor resides in the female body. In Middle Eastern countries, specifically Egypt and Jordan, there is a market for hymenorrhaphy, or hymen reconstruction (Jehl, 1999). This surgery is a way for women to restore or repair the physical component of virginity in a woman's body. A popular custom in Arab weddings is for the groom to show his family and friends the blood stained sheet from the bride and groom's wedding bed. By doing so, the groom is confirming to the family and friends that his bride was, in fact, a virgin and her hymen was intact, as evident by the bleeding. However, not all women bleed during their first sexual act, and some women do not have hymens at all. Some Arab women have engaged in premarital sex. Therefore, there is a surgery to repair or restore the hymen. So on her wedding night, the young woman would bleed, the sheet with blood will be shown, and there would be no question of her virginity and therefore no question of her honor. There was no mention of honor residing anywhere on the male body. However, for women, there is a distinct physical marker of virginity that men do not have. Due to this marker of virginity residing in the female body, it seemed that women are the owners and

maintainers of physical honor as its physical construct resides in their body alone.

> And like I remember she would take me to the doctor to check on me and stuff
> like that and I'm like "What?" And I remember the doctor just used to tell her like
> "You're daughter can not only be a virgin if she had sex." And she was like, so
> the doctor would explain to her. Even if her hymen is broken, she's still a virgin,
> but it's not from sex, like it's not from, you know what I mean? But God forbid,
> no, my mom had to check on me. I wasn't even allowed to use tampons.

> You should maintain your honor and your family's honor by staying a virgin until
> you are married. But it isn't just your family's honor, it's ours too! If had a
> daughter, I would teach her about honor and how to respect her body and stay a
> virgin and never dishonor herself by giving it before marriage.

> Her body is where her honor is. She has to protect it by making sure she is in the
> right place, at the right time, with the right people.

> A lot of my friends were told that their husbands would know if they weren't
> virgins. They were also threatened with being taken to the doctor to check. I don't
> think you can do that in America, but you can in Egypt. It is a pretty common
> surgery, you are in and out in 30 minutes and you can be a virgin again and no
> one has to know.

Pattern 1.2 Self-respect. There was a shared idea within the co-researchers that

respect in the Arab community started with one's self. If you do not respect yourself, no

one will respect you. The concept of self-respect came up during the discussion of honor

as a way to honor yourself. This was a different focus on the concept of honor, in that

honor was something that was important to the individual first. Honoring oneself

translated to loving oneself. This idea seemed to bleed over into honor and respect in

regards to the family. If the individual loves and respects themselves enough to act

honorably, then their actions would not dishonor the family. If you honor yourself and

your family, the natural conclusion would be you respect yourself and your family. It seems that the dignity of the individual is tied into the dignity of the family, and the only

way to maintain the dignity of the family is to maintain your self-respect.

> The value of the person should correlate with the value that they have for
> themselves. Honor means that you value yourself. You value your family and you
> value your reputation and theirs. That quality of honor is important to me. It is
> important because it increases the value of the individual.

> Early on, my parents taught me the relationship between respect and honor. Self-
> respect, respect for your family members and respect for your community, culture
> and religion brought you and your family honor. And your honor is to be guarded
> and protected because once lost, it's incredibly difficult to regain.

> I just want to emphasize that if you don't honor yourself, no one will. If you
> disrespect yourself, everyone will feel they can disrespect you. Male, female,
> whatever.

> What honor means to me is to have respect for myself and to be respected, to feel
> like I belong, to respect those around me and to feel accepted while being proud
> of who I am.

Pattern 1.3 Being a "good girl". This reoccurring pattern was brought up as a

way to behave, a preferred way to behave. There was a mention of parents often referring

to this "good girl" behavior, but also of husband's preferring this "good girl" behavior.

For the parents, a "good girl" listened to her parents, helped around the house, did well in

school, and was modest in her actions and clothing. For a potential husband, a "good girl"

was a girl who was a virgin and was not known to have a reputation for inappropriate

behavior.

Socially, it seemed that honor and being a "good girl" seemed to go hand in hand.

Sexual promiscuity and being a "good girl" did not. To be a "good girl" meant you went

to school and got good grades. It meant you obeyed your parents. It meant you did not

date and you remained a virgin until you married. If you were a female who dated, was

disobedient, or had premarital sex, you were a "bad girl," a girl no one wanted.

I thought, "Okay, if I touched a boy, oh my god, I'm not a good girl anymore."

My husband was a close friend before we got married. He knew everything about me. What did he know? I was a good girl. I didn't have boyfriends. I loved my parents. I did well in school. He has told me numerous times, "I know you, in and out." I want that transparency in my marriage. Maintaining my honor helped me attain that. I value myself and he very much values me for it.

The girls had to be "good" girls. So, growing up I didn't do what other girls normally did. We couldn't go with dates, with boys. Because we were girls.

But for me, honor is what makes me a good girl, essentially. Good to marry, to have as a daughter, good person in general.

He went on to both yell at me and praise me for not being the one talking to the boy. "I can't let you go to the movies anymore, you might talk to boys and do things. You are a good girl; I saw you waiting for me to pick you up." I was embarrassed for my potential bad behavior but also felt like a good girl because in the moment he pulled up I wasn't talking to anyone, male or female.

Pattern 1.4 Modesty. The co-researchers also brought up modesty in the

discussion of honor. Many had expressed the thought that to dress modestly was a way to

maintain one's honor. Most of the co-researchers are Muslim and do wear the veil (*hijab*)

when out in public. The *Hijab*, or the veil, is usually worn covering the hair in the

Levantine countries. The face is exposed fully, but the neck and chest are covered.

Muslims in the region do not exclusively use the veil; even the Christian co-researchers

expressed the importance of modesty. They do not veil but they also do not wear

revealing clothing, as that seems to be inappropriate and it would affect their honor.

In Arab culture, the body of the woman is not something for everyone to see.

Upon observation, the co-researchers did dress modestly: mostly in longer sleeves and

pants. Four co-researchers did wear the *hijab*. In the Quran, it is stated that

And say to the believing women that they should lower their gaze and guard their modesty; that they should not display their beauty and ornaments except what (must ordinarily) appear thereof; that they should draw their veils over their

bosoms and not display their beauty except to their husbands, their fathers, their
husband's fathers, their sons, their husbands' sons, their brothers or their brothers'
sons, or their sisters' sons (Quran 24:31, Oxford World's Classics Edition).

It makes it clear to the female Muslim that she is to dress modestly and that her

beauty should only be shown to specific male members of her family. The bible also

mentions the command to dress modestly:

> Likewise, I want women to adorn themselves with proper clothing, modestly and
> discreetly, not with braided hair and gold or pearls or costly garments, but rather
> by means of good works, as is proper for women making a claim to godliness (1
> Timothy 2:9).

It would appear that though the co-researchers were from two different religious

backgrounds, Islam and Christianity, the common religious command of modesty had

permeated the Arab culture. So much so, that it would be correlated with honorable

behavior in itself.

> I feel at a disadvantage sometimes. I am Muslim, so I dress modestly. I do not veil
> but I feel that because I value my honor and don't show the world everything, I
> maybe don't get a job that a woman in a short skirt gets.

> I love to wear my veil and cover myself. It is a way to show the world, "No, you
> can't look at all I have. That is just for me and my husband." It is a wonderful and
> protective thing to be modest in your clothing. It is more than honorable.

> Hijab is an outward showing of honor. To veil is to be honorable in Muslim
> culture. Modesty is highly valued and an honorable trait in a woman.

> I just don't show everything. I am Christian so I don't have to cover my face or
> hair. But I wear shirts that aren't low cut. I don't wear short shorts. That's not
> ladylike, that's not Christian.

Theme 2: Social Status

Many of the co-researchers mentioned how one's social status would be affected

by the status of their honor. Social status plays a role in who is and who is not appropriate

to marry. As marriage is very important in Arab culture, one can understand the importance placed on your social standing, as it directly affects whether or not you can marry and who would be interested in marrying you. Entire families can be affected socially by the actions of one member: specifically, one female member. Her actions can influence the marriageability of all the females in her family, immediate and extended.

Since the entire family is affected by the actions and therefore honor of the individual, it makes sense that families as a whole are quite concerned with honor, of the individual and as a family. Families still have a significant say in Arab culture as to whom their children marry. Therefore, if a girl were deemed not honorable based on her social behaviors, then she would no longer be invited to social gatherings, and later would not be approved of as marriage material. Her social standing determines her ability, and other female family members, to marry, if at all.

Pattern 2.1 Being judged. There was a great importance placed on how one is perceived in Arab culture. If one is perceived to be honorable, then there would be no problem in social circles and later in regards to marriage. The community would not judge the individual harshly. The individual would be perceived as one who would be a good wife, good daughter in law, and later down the line, a good mother who would teach her daughters how to act honorably.

However, if the individual were perceived to be behaving dishonorably, they would be immediately and harshly judged by the community. This individual would not be someone welcome at social gatherings, be considered for marriage, and the family from which she came would be judged. The co-researchers were a mix of Muslim and Christian Arab Americans and co-researchers from both religions expressed concern over being judged by their communities in regards to their honor and behavior.

I protected myself and my parents protected me by instilling the importance of honor in me from my childhood. I never brought other people's judgment down on their heads because of my actions.

How you are perceived is everything. It can make or break your reputation. And when your reputation is all you have, you should guard it.

You have honor and it is easy to lose with certain behaviors or actions. To keep it, you maintain good behaviors. Don't put yourself in bad positions, where people can question you or your morals.

It was for my protection. Protection from boys, from sex, from being judged by society.

I am not my body and I come from a culture that places importance on the female body in such a way that it is socially crippling for the whole family.

Pattern 2.2 Being ostracized. In addition to being judged, co-researchers mentioned repeatedly that once you were judged for dishonorable behavior, the community often followed with ostracizing the family and the individual who was deemed dishonorable. Seemingly, innocuous social gatherings, such as a weekly coffee date among family friends would become off limits to those whose behavior or their children's behavior was deemed dishonorable. It could extend to other social gatherings such as weddings, which is a huge blow to the Arab individual. Most marriages begin at another Arab individual's wedding.

For example, large groups of families meet and socialize, information is passed and processed. To be ostracized from this meet and greet would be detrimental to the marriage process for any young girl and her family. The individual's actions affected the family socially not only in that there would be gossip, but a real exclusion from social activities and events. These social activities and events would determine the course of the young girl's life and the lives of her female family members.

You are a good girl or young woman because you don't want to be socially an outcast because of your behavior and how it reflects on your person.

Your shame is contagious to your family though. It affects them socially. People won't talk to them, their kids won't hang out with your kids, and when you get older you aren't an acceptable option for marriage. So, I guess their fears were warranted, shame is contagious.

Your social group in Arab culture indicates to society what type of person you are, which indicates what type of person you can marry. It informs your place essentially.

Maintaining "clean" image or reputation is important to me and I think most Arab women because it directly affects your social standing which directly affects your marriage prospects which directly affects your family.

It is kind of a big deal if you don't get invited to a wedding or a birth celebration. It's like most eligible bachelor time. You get to scope out who is around, oh is she single or he single? That kind of thing. Then your mom can send an aunt over and get the scoop. But if you don't get invited, you miss all that. All those opportunities to meet who you are going to marry.

Pattern 2.3 Education. Co-researchers mentioned another, if not smaller, way a woman could maintain her honor. It was indicated by the co-researchers that education plays a large role in Arab culture and has the ability to make a woman more honorable. Education is initially something that keeps the young girl out of trouble in the eyes of the parents. If she is keeping her mind on books, her mind would not have the chance to wander to boys and therefore, give the young girl the chance to behave dishonorably.

As a young Arab woman gets older, education becomes something of an ornament on her person. It accentuates her many attributes. She may be beautiful, kind, obedient, but also she is educated. It does not have the importance of virginity however, an educated virgin is highly valued, and co-researchers were very much encouraged by their parents to go to school and get an education, in that it would make them even more desirable when it came time to marry.

Focus on school. Education, education, education was my father's mantra.

Education is hugely tied into honor in Arab culture. When your daughter gets into college it's a big deal, but for my dad we got into ivy league schools. Which was huge for us but also huge for him. That meant my parents did a good job as parents, in our culture.

Education was important but I mean there was the pressure to do well. School was a way to distinguish yourself. So if you did well, that was a way to honor your parents.

I like to think of a woman's characteristics in Arab culture like the Christmas tree. All the things about her are the ornaments. The balls and lights and candy canes. Beauty is the lights, candy canes and balls are like her wit and loyalty and education. But the star on that tree, the tops is virginity. Everything else about her is an ornament, nice and adds to the whole picture, but not the top.

Pattern 2.4 Importance of a "good marriage". Marriage is highly encouraged in Arab culture, as it is the acceptable way to have sex and eventually children. In fact, in Islam, it is part of your religious duty to marry. It is stated in the Quran that Muslims are to marry. "And wed the single among you" (Quran 24:32, Oxford World's Classics Edition). It is rare in Arab Muslims communities to find a single older male or female. Somehow, some way, there will be some family member who suggests a friend or acquaintance who is also single.

In Christian Arab communities, there is less pressure to marry and have children, but in the more religiously observant households, the pressure is still there. Christian Arabs will cite the Bible in regards to the importance of marriage and children, "Be fruitful and increase in number; fill the earth and subdue it" (Genesis 1:28a). The only condition in Orthodox Christianity is that it is only socially acceptable to have sex and children if you are married, in Arab culture. Understanding this, it is clear that if someone would behave in an inappropriate or dishonorable manner, and it affected their marriage

prospects, how it could in turn affect the individual and the family.

> We have had some female family members act a certain way or dress
> provocatively or have inappropriate relationships. Their actions directly dishonor
> them but also extended to us. If my female family members were allowed to keep
> going with their dishonorable actions, it may have affected my ability to marry.
> My husband may not have wanted a woman from a family where some of the
> girls are viewed as damaged goods. Not virgins. Suspected of being impure.

> My family's honor rests me on and my sisters. Our behavior, our actions. I can
> affect their marriage choices with my actions and visa versa. Why would I hurt
> their chances or my chances with bad choices? It's hard but it's worth it.

> When you are even older, of marriage age, your honor affects who wants to marry
> you. It can broaden or limit your options. If you were a girl who dated and was
> known to be around boys, your honor or virginity is questioned so who would
> want to marry a girl like that?

> It is really important to not wait too long to get married. If you are older, no one
> will want you. So, marriage in your twenties is preferred. That way, you can have
> your education, your husband can have his job, and you can have kids all inside
> the marriage and everything is good. Most desirable outcome right there.

Theme 3: Parental role. While this study focuses on the experience of honor

among first generation Levantine Arab American women, each of the co-researchers

mentioned the role their parents played in their experience of honor. There were four

particular patterns mentioned and each had vivid descriptions, memories that were crystal

clear and had a strong tie to the co-researcher's experience of honor.

Pattern 3.1: Lack of communication between parent and child. In this pattern,

the co-researchers felt that there was a complete lack of communication on the part of the

parent and on the part of the child. On the behalf of the parent, the co-researchers felt that

there was little to no explanation as to why the rules were what they were. The co-

researchers felt that the parent never informed them that their future, the future of their siblings, socially and otherwise, would be at stake. On the behalf of the co-researchers, they felt that they could not communicate their feelings to their parents, for fear of punishment or shame.

It was discussed in the interviews that the co-researchers would have appreciated an explanation as to why the rules were as they were. This lack of an explanation as to why the co-researchers had to protect their honor, lead to anger, mistrust, and resentment on both sides of the parent child relationship. Something, the co-researchers explained, that could have been avoided by merely communicating to their children.

> Now that I'm grown up and realize what it is, I think my mom came out to tell me about it in a wrong way. She didn't really explain to me how it works.

> There's just no communication. She didn't tell me why we're not allowed to have sex. It was just like you'll die; it will kill you if you do that. That's why I I'm like "What?" you know.

> I want more open communication with me and my children than I had with my parents. I was scared to talk to my parents, to express my feelings about things like boys and sex.

> So, yea when I have kids, I will be strict but I want to make sure they communicate with me. I didn't have that with my parents. I do now but not when I was young. And I think that would have helped a lot in our relationship. They never explained why. WHY do I have to stay home when all my friends get to go out? WHY is my virginity so important? It was just, you won't be able to get married.

Pattern 3.2 Forbidding socializing with boys/forbidding sex. The main goal of all the co-researcher's parents was to preserve the virginity of their daughters. There was one common method to do this that all the co-researcher's parents employed. They did their best to keep their daughters, once they reached a certain age; it was different for each one, away from males. The co-researcher's parents all would forbid any activity or location where the co-researchers may encounter boys or could possibly have an opportunity to have sex. Activities such as going to the movie theater, parties, and after school programs were off limits, no matter how innocuous they seemed.

Each co-researcher had a specific memory regarding a conversation or an activity that was deemed inappropriate by her parents, specifically because boys could be or would be present, and there would not be an adult to supervise. This limited the co-researchers from participating in most school and extracurricular activities. Organized sports, female only teams, were allowed; however, intermural sports with integrated teams were not. Activities in afterschool programs were not allowed, as there were not enough adults to supervise the mixed boys and girls. This limited the co-researchers in regards to extracurricular activities.

> My mom knew that school ended at 2:30 or something. I came home at 6 o'clock because I went to an after school program. I explained to her like "Listen, Thursday I'm going to after school." She used to think that after school was the most dangerous sex infested place. She said you just want to go because there's boys and whatever, you know? And I'm like, "What do you mean? I don't care about the boys. I want to go play soccer."

> Every time she- like I couldn't even ask her for anything. It would definitely be a no. Can I go to the movies? No. Can I do something else? Only in the house.

> No one would want to marry a girl who was considered dirty, used, damaged. And the way you get to be any of those things was to do unsupervised, unapproved things, or outings with boys or men.

> I was 13 and my cousin and I were at the movies. And my dad came to pick us up and she was talking to a boy. We got in the car and he started lecturing her but also yelling. "You can't talk to boys now, you girls are too big. Boys don't want to be your friend. What if something happened to you? What if he did something?"

> Once I was in high school, my guidance counselor asked me to join a club or two to boost my appeal to colleges. I had straight A's so I assumed my mom would let me do debate or something like that. She said no. There were boys on debate and one only teacher in charge. How could the teacher keep an eye on all of us at once? So, because it was mixed boys and girls and the student teacher ratio was one to thirty, I couldn't do any clubs. It was fine; I still got into a good school.

But I wonder if maybe if I seemed more well rounded, could I have gotten into like a Harvard?

Pattern 3.3 Family rules. Each participant mentioned that her family had rules for their behaviors, their movements, and their social interactions. Clothing was a controlled area, which most people would take for granted, what you wear is usually your choice. However, the co-researcher's families had rules as to what was appropriate in regards to honor and what was not. Talking to boys was also an often-mentioned rule among the co-researchers, as something that was a verbally expressed rule and over emphasized.

Co-researchers mentioned that the family rules did not really apply to their brothers. The males in the family did not have to come home at a certain time, the parents did not seem to care who they socialized with, or if they dated. While it is a double standard, it makes sense as the girls have their virginity to protect and the boys do not. The boys are the ones who turn into adult males who want virgin wives. Therefore, it is acceptable if they are not virgins.

> And it's funny, sometimes the bad behavior is imagined. "I know you are talking to boys on the phone!' "I know you are talking to boys at school!" I always felt like I had to be on guard. Like my honor was constantly under attack. It was kind of ridiculous. I was always thought to be breaking the rules.

> There was never an explanation, about the rules, the social customs, the religion that somehow gets tied up into it.

> There were a lot of rules growing up. Who you could talk to, play with, spend time with. Even what you wear.

> My brother got to do whatever he wanted. I can't tell you how many times I would bring him up to my parents, asking why he got to do this or that. "He's a boy" or "It's different" was all I got. Those were the rules in our house. Be good because you are a girl. He can be bad because he is a boy.

Pattern 3.4 Guilt. Each of the co-researchers mentioned feeling guilt for their actions that caused their parents disappointment with their behavior. If the parent were embarrassed, it would cause the co-researcher to feel incredibly guilty. Honorable behavior was something you did not feel guilty for and so in order to avoid that emotion, the co-researchers would avoid dishonorable behavior.

All of the co-researchers had parents who came here from the Levant in the Middle East. Most arrived in the United States with very little money and did what they had to in order to succeed. In knowing that, it makes sense that the co-researcher feels incredible guilt when they disappoint or shame their parents. There is a weight on the co-researcher's mind, an understanding that your parent did so much for you, sacrificed for you. Your only job as a daughter in an Arab family is to do what your parents ask. When you do not, you hurt the parent who left their home for a better life for their children, who immigrated to a strange and scary place for you to have opportunities they did not.

> I am a big girl now and my behavior has to be that of a lady. I was 9. I felt embarrassed and upset that I had visibly disappointed my father.

> I have done things that normal teenagers did, and I remember the embarrassment on my father's face, the gossiping of other Arab people in our community. I never want to do that to him again. It makes me feel physically sick when I think of how I have disappointed and embarrassed my parents with my dishonorable behavior.

> I mean, for some women they say-, some of the people I've talked to, they say "Oh, it made them feel special." Like their parents were telling them "Oh, you're different and you're so special and don't let boys touch you and da, da, da." And that's some people's experience. But then on the other side of that, some people, it made them feel guilty for any little thing they did. Any behavior not deemed honorable would be something you felt incredibly guilty for.

> I always feel bad because my mom came here with me then my dad followed a year later. That year was the hardest of her life, she used to tell me. She was here with my aunt so they shared a one-bedroom apartment, one worked days and one worked nights. They took turns watching me. So when I acted up, when I made a

big deal about going to prom or whatever, she would yell and scream that she literally gave up her life for me to be here. To go to school and make something of myself, not wear an open dress in a limo full of boys who only wanted to have sex. She was right.

Theme 4: Shame

Shame was an integral theme in the study. It was something that occurred as a result of the co-researcher's behaviors and as a result of breaking spoken and unspoken rules. It was an emotion felt by both the co-researcher and the co-researcher's parents because of the co-researcher's behavior. It was an emotion that would cause great distress among a family and to the individual, even if it was their choice to participant in actions that would cause the family shame. Each co-researcher mentioned moments, memories, or instances of behaviors that caused them to feel shame during their lives and in regards to the experience of honor.

Pattern 4.1 Disappointing your parents. Disappointment is an emotion that the co-researchers actively tried to avoid. It appeared that due to the co-researcher's failure to meet their parent's expectations caused feelings of disappointment in the parents. The co-researchers would make personal, everyday choices based solely on the fact that they did not want their actions to cause their parents feelings of disappointment. Co-researchers mentioned an intense desire to avoid disappointing their parents, at the cost of their social life and happiness.

Each co-researcher had a memory or experience in disappointing her parents. Whether it was by breaking a rule, arguing, or doing badly in school, each co-researcher discussed the disappointment as something to be avoided and as something that could be avoided if you had behaved honorably. Some co-researcher's parents showed

disappointment emotionally and some with physical discipline.

> I am not saying my mother and father would have killed me, but there would have
> been serious consequences. I might have gotten hit. Probably have gotten hit.
> Their disappointment showed physically.

> Your honor starts in the family aspect. You are a good daughter so you don't
> shame your family. Don't disappoint your mother and father by being badly
> behaved.

> He didn't even have to say anything. He could just give you a look that said, "I'm
> disappointed." It would be the end.

> I never want to disappoint my mom. It makes me want to cry when I think of how
> hurt she is when I had done something to dishonor myself or family. Her face
> would, like, crumble, it was the saddest thing. I misbehaved once, after that, it
> wasn't worth the hurt I saw on my mother's face.

Pattern 4.2 Inappropriate relationships. Inappropriate relationships were those

with males who were not related to the co-researchers and after a certain age, co-

researchers quoted that it was between the ages of 7 and 9. At this age, the co-researchers

were considered women and therefore had to act like adult women. It would make sense

that socially, it would start that young because Arab marriages are generally much

younger than Western marriages. For example, in a 2002 study on age and first time

marriage, it was found that 10% of women were married between the ages of 15-19, 52%

of women married between the ages of 20-24, and 3% were married between the ages of

35-39 (Rashad, Osman, & Roudi-Fahimi, 2005).

Friendships with males were considered inappropriate, in addition to romantic

relationships. Arab families generally do not approve of dating, as one could date for an

extended period, lose your virginity, and never end up married to that person. Therefore,

most interactions between males and females are supervised; courtships are short and arranged by the parents of both parties involved. The family pursues appropriate

relationships, or the family of the male parents meet and arrange marriages. Both parents

have to approve of the other parents, the other family, and the other potential spouse.

> When all my friends were going to the movies, I was asked over and over if boys
> were going, then once I was 13 I wasn't allowed to go to the movies anymore so
> that was that. So I knew at that age that honor was something to do with my
> interaction with boys. It seemed that only bad things happened when you
> socialized with boys so don't do it.

> We live at home while we go to school. Because school is everything. Education
> is honorable for an Arab girl. The more the better. And once we are done with
> school and have a job, we look for a husband. But through the appropriate
> avenues. We don't go to bars. We have aunts and uncles and family friends who
> know someone our age.

> We weren't allowed to date. My mother would always comment on my friends
> and all the guys they used to run through. Though it didn't seem that bad to me,
> but to her it was her pointing out, "look how many men she kissed before her
> husband, how many men did she sleep with?". It seemed silly like, even if she had
> several serious relationships before getting married, what if that was 5 guys? 6
> guys? That would be completely unacceptable in our community. So, they don't
> even open the door to the conversation on dating. It's a firm NO.

Pattern 4.3 Community rules. There is a value for independence and

individualism in Western culture that clashes deeply with the Arab community that lives

in the United States. Arab culture, as discussed by the co-researchers, seems to value the

importance of the community and its rules. The values of the community are the values of

the individual, therefore to maintain these values become the responsibility of the

individual and are enforced by rules by the families. As they were described, these rules

are in place to protect the women in the community, to protect their honor.

There were rules that were unspoken in the Arab communities of the co-

researchers. These rules governed the co-researchers' behavior and interactions. If the

rules were broken, the consequences were not only on behalf of the co-researcher, but the parents of the co-researcher would also suffer at the hands of the community, even

though they were not the ones who had broken the rules. Therefore, these community

rules were also enforced in the upbringing and lifestyles of the co-researchers and their

families.

> In Arab culture, there are spoken and unspoken rules about how a girl should behave, where her focus should be, and who she should associate with. It's interesting to me, my parents hated a certain friend of mine, she was known to be "loose" and was someone who dated. This was not acceptable in our culture; she was a great friend. But my parents did not want me socializing with her because her shame seemed to be transferrable to me? Like shame was contagious?

> My parents are good people, they are conservative. But I am aware now that any rules they imposed on me were due to society putting pressure on them. If they weren't going to suffer social consequences because of my dishonorable behavior, then they would never impose these strict rules on me. It's a vicious cycle.

> Your social circles are everything. Community is very important to us. Especially, since we are living here and not back home. Here, we have each other. And we need each other. It helps us keep our customs and traditions. So we have these like, ways to interact, that keeps everything on the up and up. Women follow a certain pattern of behavior that has been put into place by generations of our parents and grandparents. The rules are be a virgin, don't run around, go to school, be a good girl for your parents. And everyone enforces them. Every family. That is the ideal female child.

Pattern 4.4 Importance of virginity. Virginity is not a private and personal thing

in Arab culture. In fact, who is and who is not a virgin is quite publically discussed in

social circles. As it stands, the importance of virginity is a social, physical, cultural, and

even psychological component of Arab culture. Some co-researchers mentioned the

importance of virginity as a huge stressor in their lives, causing serious anxiety.

The theme of virginity as it affects the individual socially and in terms of the

familial relationship has been discussed earlier. However, the importance of virginity, in

regards to the emotion of shame felt by the family and the individual, was a large focus in regards to the co-researchers and their behaviors. All the rules, regulations, and

restrictions were focused on maintaining the co-researcher's virginity. A co-researcher's

virginity was compared to her cleanliness, and a clean wife was a desirable wife. A co-

researcher's virginity dictated her marriage choices.

> Honor means I have no personal shame, no family shame. I came to my husband
> clean. It makes me feel really good.

> To my parents, their social standing and mine depend on whether I was a virgin or
> not, which would indicate who I would be allowed to marry. They are so focused
> on virginity. Because it affects them too.

> I was scared to even kiss a boy, in case that lead to something more. I never
> wanted my virginity questioned. It was so vital to a good marriage that I couldn't
> risk it.

> The fact that a woman's virginity is even up for public discussion is mind
> boggling to American's but this is normal conversation in Arab culture. It's like
> coffee talk, gossip. I mean, it is super damaging gossip, but its…what's the word?
> For a culture that is so conservative about bodies and sex, we talk about virginity
> really loosely.

Theme 5: Looking Ahead

Each co-researcher mentioned the future, future relationships with children and

how they wanted to conduct those relationships. The patterns that emerged had largely to

do with trust, communication, respect, and independence. Each co-researcher mentioned

how they would do things differently, how they would raise any future, or current

children differently than their parents had raised them in regards to honor. There would

be independence instilled in their children, as they felt they were not given that option.

There would be communication between parent and child, a characteristic that was felt to

be missing in their own relationships with their parents. There would also be a level of trust that was not at all present in the relationships between the co-researchers and their parents.

Pattern 5.1 Trust between parent and child. The family structure in the Arab community is still a patriarchal one. The father has the responsibility in providing for the family and is the final authority. Therefore, the behavior preferred by the father is the behavior that the mother will enforce. While most of the co-researchers described their fathers as kind and loving, there was also a mention of the strictness of their father's parenting style.

The lack of trust between parent and child was a pattern that emerged in all the co-researcher's data. Lack of trust began in childhood and adolescence, and in some cases continued to adulthood. In addition, trust was something the co-researchers aspired to have with their future children, as they did not have it with their parents growing up and they felt it affected their relationship.

> I work hard to be reliable and trustworthy and keep the promises I made to my parents. Honoring myself mean honoring the relationships I have with my husband, my family members and my friends. I want my children to trust me because I feel like my parents didn't trust me and that affected our relationship.

> I feel like my mom now has FaceTime and stuff and she still doesn't trust us and she still tries to call us on FaceTime to see where we are. It's like "Mom, I'm married, what are you doing?" But I see that even now, she still doesn't trust me. I don't want that with my kids. I want there to be a trust between us. I trust them and they trust me.

> My mother and father were both strict, but my dad more than my mom. I would sneak in late and pray to God my dad didn't catch me, but if my mom caught me I was less scared. I could negotiate with my mom. No way I would get away with that with my dad.

> My father and I would, and still argue a lot about what he thought was acceptable behavior. I'm a grown woman now and he doesn't like that I have a drink with dinner. I'm 30! But even in my teens, my dad was super strict and conservative.

My mom would always defer to his judgment when I asked to go do something. And it was always no.

Pattern 5.2 Independence. In Arab families, it is expected that the children are to defer to older family members in regards to behavior. Co-researchers described it as the individual's responsibility to respect the parents and the family enough to put the needs and wants of the family before their own needs and wants. Therefore, there is a conflict in the Western cultural value of independence and the patriarchal system in Arab culture when it comes to the independence of their children. However, co-researcher's described independence was something they aspired to, attainable through education. If one had independence, they were no longer held to the rules of their families or communities. It was also something the co-researchers wanted for their children.

> With my children, I want them to have higher expectations for themselves. To value themselves. Not 100% because I want them to, but because THEY want to.

> I kind of view women now where they should rebel. I think they should take pride in their independence, and who they are. I don't believe in anything that a man is better than anyone.

> That's why when I was able to get a job, I got my own job, my own money, I bought a car, I didn't want anybody to tell me you can't do this, you can't do that. My independence meant that my parents didn't have any say in what I did, not even financially.

> In our family, I could never have moved out when I was 20 something. In order to move out, I had to be married. You go from your father's house to your husband's house. That was the only acceptable way to leave. Otherwise, you live with and take care of your parents.

> It was annoying when all my friends were dorming in college and had all this freedom. They would come and go. Hang out, go to parties. I didn't have that option, I was no way allowed to live on my own. Too little supervision, my parents were horrified when they found out your RA is another student just a year older! So, they were like "No, no, you stay home. We will buy you a new car."

Pattern 5.3 Respect for your family. Family lies at the center of Arab society, in all aspects. Therefore, there is a distinction in that one's behavior whether positive or negative, is directly tied to whether or not one respects their family. The co-researchers described it as a linking between you and your family; these familial relationships are based on respect. One's honor was tied to one's respect for their family. Respect for your parents and their culture, respect for your parents and what they provide for you, love for you and your love for them.

It would make sense to describe the concept of respect for your parents as a way to show them you loved them. You show your affections by being respectful towards them and their wishes in regards to you and your behavior. If you respected your family, there would be no dishonorable behavior that would disappoint, upset, shame, or bring judgment on themselves or their family. Your behavior has a ripple effect in these communities, so does your respect for your family.

> I am not just acting for myself in my actions, I am acting for my family. My actions don't just affect me, they affect my family. Honor was important to my family so therefore honor was important to me.

> My mother would tell me that if I was promiscuous that it just showed her that I didn't love or respect her. If I did respect her, I would respect the family and act right.

> "How could you do this to me, to your father? We give you everything and you don't give us the respect we deserve." I would hear that all the time. Any time I did something that was not honorable for a girl. It could be walking to the corner store with a group of friends, some of whom were boys. It seems so silly now but in choosing to do that, I was disrespecting my parents.

> With Arab girls and their fathers, love is respect and respect is love. It is almost like you don't love your parents if you don't respect them. It sounds dramatic but that is how it is.

Pattern 5.4 Relationships with children/future children. The co-researchers

mentioned often during the interviews that they were going to raise their children

differently than their parents raised them. When pressed on the differences, trust was a

component that they felt was missing in the relationships with their own parents. They

felt that their parents did not trust their judgment and displayed their distrust by enforcing

rules without an explanation. The co-researchers understood their parent's lack of trust,

some citing friends who openly lied to their parents, however felt that their parents had

instilled values in them that they themselves valued. These values would govern their

behavior, but their parents did not trust them to do so on their own.

The topic of trust lead to the co-researchers explaining that there was little to no

communication between the co-researchers and their parents. The co-researchers who had

children, two co-researchers did, mentioned that they were going to be more

communicative with their children than their parents were with them. They will still

emphasize honor and its importance, but the missing component of communication will

be an integral part of the relationships. This concept of communication was just as

important to those co-researchers who did not have children yet.

> Now I understand like when I have children I'm going to explain to them "Okay,
> don't have sex because, you know, this or that. I'm going to let them do whatever
> they need to. They want to go out with their friends, they're allowed go out with
> their friends, but I'm going to explain to them that this is not what you're
> supposed to do.

> I just want to know that they're telling me the truth. I want to build that
> connection with my kids where they're telling me the truth and I'm okay with
> whatever it is.

> I think to really make sure my children understand how important honor is, I need
> them to be able to talk to me about things that would affect their choices to be
> honorable, especially girls.

At my age, I am 34, it is now about how I conduct myself and how I raise my children. NOW, my honor is dependent on my children's behavior! I find myself telling my 5-year-old daughter things like "Don't do that, good girls don't do that."

They just didn't trust us. There were other kids, wild kids, and we were just like them. So we needed rules and regulations. There was no thought of, maybe my daughter doesn't want to run around and have sex with everyone? Maybe she is just as conservative as I am? No, they made the decision for me because they didn't trust me to make the right choice when it was entirely up to me.

Creative Synthesis

The first generation Levantine Arab American women struggles with the concept of honor on a daily basis. It is part of their lives, on all levels, on a familial level, relational, social, cultural, and religious level. The lived experience of honor includes one's anger, shame, guilt, resentment, and understanding of one's own value system. It includes the developing of one's own new definition of honor, one that may differ from the definition laid out by the co-researcher's parents. Honor is divisive and inclusive in Arab culture. It separates individuals and families from society, but can help maintain the already existing and strong family bond.

Honor is a multifaceted experience as it is experienced by the first generation Arab American woman. There are many moving parts, each connecting and affecting the other, and affecting the experience as a whole. The experience of honor begins for the first generation Arab American woman, as a young girl. Her virginity is her and her family's most prized possession. Any hint of a loss of her virginity affects her and her family's social standing, and even further can affect her ability to marry well. Therefore, her parents will restrict her activities and her behaviors so that she will rarely, if ever, be in a position to lose her virginity, or in a place where society can question it. As she moves into adulthood, the experience changes slightly. Now, her honor is maintained by instilling the same values into her children, the importance of virginity, marriage, and social standing are still relevant. However, these co-researchers are changing the way in which they instill these values into their future or current children. Honor is still important. However, the why of its importance is now part of the conversation between parent and child. A conversation that was never held between the co-researchers and their parents.

The primary researcher has always felt a tug between her individualistic nature and her traditional culture. Both are important to her, but it always seemed that her traditional culture would be given preference. Her individual choices would affect her current life and future life; therefore, it would make sense to do what would be best for her overall. Many of the co-researchers shared this sentiment that the greater good was more important than the individual's wants and needs. In researching the experience of honor among first generation Levantine Arab American women, the primary researcher was able to not only understand the experience but also to see her co-researchers making the same life choices she did and for the same reasons. She discovered that the experience she had was shared by other women in her community and that they used the same language and expressions when talking about it.

The primary researcher struggled with feelings of betrayal to her culture during the study. She did not want her community to perceive her study as damning in regards to their customs. However, after interviewing several co-researchers and hearing about their experiences, seeing the similarities, she was able to feel confident in the study and her ability to convey the experience clearly to those inside and outside the community.

The primary researcher may have begun the study with co-researchers between the ages of 25-35, but as the study was conducted, it was found that the experience of honor begins at birth. The phrase "It's a Girl!" kicks off a lifetime of understanding your sex and how it affects you and your family. Honor is not an individual characteristic; it is a communal one. It starts with the female and ends with the family.

Exemplary Portraits

The primary researcher reviewed each of the co-researchers' depictions of the experience of honor. The primary researcher then chose three co-researchers who demonstrated the experience of the group as a whole. Verbatim quotes and journal entries are used to illustrate clearly the selected co-researchers' lived experience of honor. The names of the co-researchers were removed and replaced with numbers to protect the privacy of the co-researchers.

Portrait 1: Participant 2

The first portrait describes Participant 2's lived experience of honor as a first generation Levantine Arab American woman. Participant 2 was a 34-year-old married woman who works in finance. She is very happy in her marriage, has one child, and currently does not have plans for any more children in the near future, as she is focusing on her career. She grew up with her family; she is a practicing Muslim. The primary researcher chose Participant 2 because she provided a clear and descriptive understanding of the experience of honor as it related to virginity. She begins her story with her first memory of honor:

> I was very young and I was sitting on an uncle's lap. Later that day my mother told me not to do that anymore. After that, I was not really encouraged to sit with

my dad and uncles during family events. It was always, "come sit with the women, you are a big girl now" I was maybe 8 or 9. That was considered a big girl. I guess I was. It made me feel proud. Who doesn't want to be a big girl? You think it comes with more privilege but it actually came with more restrictions. What you wore, who you socialized with, etc. Because now, you have something men want. And I can see this now with my daughter. She is 8 and I see girls her age dressing way older than they are. That is terrifying to me.

At a young age, the separation between males and females becomes common. It would seem strange to American families to do so, but in Arab society, it is another way to ensure nothing untoward ever happened. As a young girl, her virginity was emphasized as the most important part of her; it determined her whole worth. The value of her virginity was important to her family, her community, and herself. She explains it as such:

> As a woman, honor is your whole life. You learn about it from when you are young until you are married. And then even, when you have children, it comes back up again when you have female children. I learned that I had value and worth. But it was all tied into my virginity. My value and worth was based on whether I was a virgin or not. Or even if I was suspected of not being a virgin. It was negative because I think there is more to my worth than my virginity. Positive because I had so much value placed on my virginity, that I didn't run around and date a lot. I didn't sleep around.

Participant 2 discussed the importance of honor in regards to marriage and how it changes how men see you in Arab culture. She valued her virginity and so did her husband when she got married, it was a characteristic that was looked for by her husband.

> Honor is a very important thing to a woman. And to me. I think that my virginity was crucial. If I wasn't a virgin when I got married my husband wouldn't respect me as much as he does. He wouldn't value me. Whatever men say, that it doesn't matter if a girl is a virgin, it does. No one wants a girl who has slept with many men. Like that game that school teachers play to show the impact of bullying? Squeeze all the toothpaste out of the tube, then ask the kids to put it back. They can't! Honor and virginity are important to me because they are important in my culture. It is how it is. My family's honor rests me on and my sisters. Our behavior, our actions. I can affect their marriage choices with my actions and visa versa. Why would I hurt their chances or my chances with bad choices? It's hard

but it's worth it. My husband was a close friend before we got married. He knew everything about me. What did he know? I was a good girl. I didn't have boyfriends. I loved my parents. I did well in school. He has told me numerous times, "I know you, in and out." I want that transparency in my marriage. Maintaining my honor helped me attain that. I value myself and he very much values me for it.

Participant 2 also stressed the importance of her virginity to her husband in regards to how he wanted his children raised. This shared value system spills into any future children that they may have together. And when they had their first child, a girl, her husband was confident in her honor that she would raise their daughter in the same way, with the same values and importance placed on honor and virginity.

My husband also valued my virginity in that, he knew I would raise my female children with honor also. In our culture, another reason a man would prefer a wife who is a virgin is because if he has daughters, he also wants them to be good girls and not run around. So, he married me, knowing how conservative I was. I have a daughter now and she is my entire world. And I make sure she knows she has to be careful, as she gets older I will emphasize to her how important her virginity it. How much it matters when you want to get married.

Participant 2 married her husband after a brief six-month engagement. This may seem quick but it is not uncommon in Arab culture to have a brief engagement. Having known her husband socially for many years before that allowed for the parents to agree quickly as to whether this was a good match. As her husband's family knew all they needed to know about her and her family, the decision was easy. Participant 2 also discussed her views on premarital sex and how it conflicted with her parent's rules and cultural norms. She obeyed their rules growing up but she did have her own reservations and qualms with their conservative rules.

Why couldn't I socialize with boys? Why couldn't I date? Why couldn't I have sex if I wanted to? It is a really old mentality that women have to be virgins in Arab culture. It's 2015. My parents were conservative but I wasn't and still am not. And if I did any of those things, why would I have to be judged by our society? Why

112

should that determine my value to my future husband? But it does. It's so medieval. For me I thought, what if I didn't want to get married? What if I wanted to have sex? But I could never say that to my parents. My mother would have a stroke.

Participant 2 describes herself as a practicing Muslim but not as religiously conservative as her parents are. She is a self-described moderate and describes her parents as more orthodox when it comes to Islam:

> My parents were very much people of the book. The Quran was everything to them. Any question that needed answering could be answered by the holy book. I am not that black and white. I feel like we live in the modern age, we need to have a gray area to live in. Not everything is as easy as yes or no. Virgin or whore. I grew up like that, with those strict lines. I don't want that for my daughter, but I also don't want her labeled if she makes a mistake when she is growing up.

Participant 2 has lived as the model Arab American daughter. She obeyed her parents growing up; she did well in school and went to a good college. She remained a virgin and therefore was able to marry a young man from a good family. She maintains her career and her family life. Participant 2 realized during the interview that her current life situation was directly connected to the choices she had made growing up; choices, which all had to do with her honor and virginity.

> Thinking back on it now, I always say that I am so lucky that I married a good man. I am so lucky to have a good job. When in all honesty, it wasn't luck, it was me. I did this for myself. I was a good girl, a smart girl. I was a virgin, that's why I have a good husband who values me. I did well in school, that's why I have a good job. I valued myself and now other people value me because of it.

Portrait 2: Participant 3

Participant 3 was a 29-year-old single woman. She has no children and has never been married, though she is looking. She works in education. The second portrait describes Participant 3's lived experience of honor as a first generation Levantine Arab

American woman. Simple, childish gestures and excitement could cause feelings of

shame and being upset on the behalf of the parents. Her experience of honor is directly

related to how her honor affected her and her family socially. Her first experience of

honor was described in the following way:

> I remember being picked up at school in grade school. My father always wore a
> black leather jacket and ran up to a man, who I thought was my father in that type
> of jacket and I jumped on his back. He turned around and it wasn't my father. I
> was quickly placed on the ground by the gentleman and heard my dad yelling for
> me across the parking lot. I got yelled at several times about not jumping on men
> and it was *eib,* fresh and not appropriate behavior. I explained to my father that I
> had mistaken that man for him and he firmly told me I shouldn't even be jumping
> on him. I am a big girl now and my behavior has to be that of a lady. I was 9. I
> felt embarrassed and upset that I had visibly disappointed my father. I think back
> on it now that maybe it wasn't disappointment on his face I was reading, but
> maybe sadness. I was growing up and there were a new set of dangers before me.
> The dangers of sex and pregnancy. The dangers of a tarnished reputation. The
> dangers of not having marriage prospects because of my behavior. At that point
> on, I was constantly made aware of these dangers and the effects they would have
> on my life, my future.

The co-researcher's awareness of their honor and its role in their life begins at an

early age. It is made clear to the co-researcher through verbal and non verbal rules that

there is a particular way to behave, a preferred way to behave. Participant 3 was chosen

by the primary researcher because she provided a clear and descriptive understanding of

the experience of honor as it related to society and social issues as a result of dishonor:

> I think it's like I don't want to embarrass my parents with my socially
> unacceptable behavior. In Arab culture, there are spoken and unspoken rules
> about how a girl should behave, where her focus should be, and who she should
> associate with. It's interesting to me, my parents hated a certain friend of mine,
> she was known to be "loose" and was someone who dated. This was not
> acceptable in our culture; she was a great friend. But my parents did not want me
> socializing with her because her shame seemed to be transferrable to me? Like
> shame was contagious? Maybe they thought her bad behavior would rub off on
> me. Your shame is contagious to your family though. It affects them socially.
> People won't talk to them, their kids won't hang out with your kids, and when

you get older you aren't an acceptable option for marriage. So, I guess their fears were warranted, shame is contagious.

My parents are good people, they are conservative. But I am aware now that any rules they imposed on me were due to society putting pressure on them. If they weren't going to suffer social consequences because of my dishonorable behavior, then they would never impose these strict rules on me. It's a vicious cycle. I am not my body and I come from a culture that places importance on the female body in such a way that it is socially crippling for the whole family.

A family's good name was everything. Participant 3 discussed the importance of

the family name as one that can make or break a person, socially. And honor was how

one maintained their family's good name. Participant 3 described dishonor as a soiling of

the individual's name and the family's name:

You should maintain your honor and your family's honor by staying a virgin until you are married. But it isn't just your family's honor, it's ours too! It's also a promise to us, ourselves, is also to do with honor. You honor your promise to yourself, the same person you marry, or your tribe or your family. This is basically Honor means to me and Arabs in general. It's about respect. For you and your family, your community. Never soiling your name or your family name or tribe name or religion. Your chastity or your honor is everything for a young girl. Anything that can cast doubt on that chastity or honor can soil your name, your family's name.

I remember being at a wedding and watching my cousin dance and dance. She was so beautiful. I smiled at her while she twirled around, she was 16. I watched as everyone in the room stared at her but not in the same way I was. I was looking at her with love and admiration. The rest of the room was looking at her with disgust; her mother embarrassingly pushed her off the dance floor. They packed up and were out the door before the cake had been cut. On the drive home, my parents in the car told me, you saw how embarrassed your aunt was? Who is going to want to marry that girl after she shook her body around for the world to see? She has always been trouble like that, always doing whatever she wants without thinking. Your poor aunt. You know, my cousin didn't marry an Arab guy. She married an American stock broker. Her poor, embarrassed mother lives with them in her own area of the huge house they live in. But our family still talks about her. How embarrassing it was for her, how she probably wasn't a virgin that's why she married an American. Who cares? Then I realize, I do. I care. How annoying is that?! I care if people think I am a virgin, I care if my family's name is muddied by gossip.

Participant 3 mentioned modesty as something that an honorable woman would have, physically on or in their person. Participant 3 identified as Muslim and wears the *hijab* or the Islamic veil. The veil in Levantine area of the Middle East is generally a piece of cloth that covers the hair, neck, and shoulders. It is not common to have a portion of the veil cover your face, as this is more the style of veil worn in the Arabian Peninsula (Saudi Arabia) and in Iran. Why would a first generation Levantine Arab American woman choose to wear the veil? In Arab culture, your body is where your honor lies, specifically your hymen. Therefore, your clothing can act as an additional layer of armor in which you can protect your honor and reputation.

> I think your honor is also something you can protect by what you wear. I love to wear my veil and cover myself. It is a way to show the world, "No, you can't look at all I have. That is just for me and my husband." It is a wonderful and protective thing to be modest in your clothing, it is more than honorable. It's a way to respect yourself in addition to your family and husband. I think of it this way; a woman dresses up to be aesthetically pleasing to whomever. And in doing so, you can attract all kinds of attention, male female whoever. In that male attention you are attracting, you are also attracting thoughts, advances etc. So, because I dress modestly I don't have to worry about any of that. I am hidden for my husband. No one can say, "oh I saw her naked". No one ever has but him.

> No one harasses me with my veil. No one cat calls me. And I live in Manhattan, the city of construction workers with no limits! They leave me alone. At work, I am not seen for my beauty or lack thereof. I am only judged on my work performance. That is kind of freeing. I know that my boss isn't checking me out. I know that men on the street aren't oogling me. I am not tempting them and they in turn do not tempt me.

Portrait 3: Participant 9

Participant 9 is a 34-year-old married woman. She works in healthcare. She identified herself as Christian. The third portrait describes Participant 9's lived experience of honor as a first generation Levantine Arab American woman. This co-researcher was chosen in regards to her experience of honor and her focus on what it would mean for the relationship with her child. In addition, Participant 9 was the only one to mention a person outside of her nuclear family to protect her honor or be concerned with her honor. This enforces the concept that a woman's honor affects her entire family; therefore, her actions would be of concern to everyone in her family no matter how far removed. Her first memory in regards to the experience of honor is as follows:

> My earliest memory in regards to honor was when I went to Syria for summer break. I was 12 years old and I was playing outside with my cousins as I usually did. My older male cousin came home from his summer job and told me that because I was a girl and it was dark I had to go back into the house and that I couldn't play with the boys that lived next t door anymore because they we were too old. I felt a lack of honor and respect and because of my stubborn nature I told him it was none of his business. He pulled me into the house by my arm. Then later apologized and said he was just worried because of the different mentality of the people in Damascus and in the area that they had lived in at the time. My first memory of honor is not a good one. It wasn't fair I thought. Now that I am older, I have daughters so I understand NOW. How you are perceived is everything. It can make or break your reputation. And when your reputation is all you have, you should guard it.

> While we had family who were Christian not Muslim, we sort of lived by the same rules. I am orthodox Christian. My religion strongly prefers the women to remain chaste. My community also enforced this preference. And my family did too. I had cousins who dated and slept around and they were the outcastes of the family. We wanted nothing to do with them. But their bad choices and wild behavior affected my family, even across an ocean. I am in America and my family friend would react to my last name like oh, we know your cousin and give this knowing look. They didn't even know me! Thankfully, my husband was able to see past the gossip and chatter. But it could have affected me, he might not have wanted me just because of what they did.

The primary researcher chose Participant 9 because she provided a clear and descriptive understanding of the experience of honor as it related to parental relationships and future relationships with her children. Participant 9 was one of the two co-researchers who had children at the time of the study and her view on honor is affected by the fact that she has a female child. She was very focused on her relationship with her daughter

and how she plans to parent her:

> I have a daughter. So I now understand my parents and the rules they had for me.
> It was for my protection. Protection from boys, from sex, from being judged by
> society. And I think that I will also be raising my daughter conservatively. She
> understands at 5 years old that her body is not for people to see, no one can touch
> her. That's normal for children her age but also, it will extend to her teen years
> and young adult hood. Her body is where her honor is. She has to protect it by
> making sure she is in the right place, at the right time, with the right people. Your
> social group in Arab culture indicates to society what type of person you are,
> which indicates what type of person you can marry. It informs your place
> essentially. She understands that even now. She came home the other day telling
> me "Mommy, such and such girl was kissing boys today during lunch. I went to
> color." I have never been so proud. Mostly because she removed herself from the
> situation. 5 years old. I didn't know to do that even at 13 years old. Protected her
> honor by not participating in shameful, dishonorable behavior.

> I love my daughter; I want to protect her no matter what. And we live in a country
> and a culture where it is acceptable to have sex early and often. But I am not
> going to raise her in American culture. I am going to raise her in Arab culture,
> where we are careful with our bodies and essentially our hearts. We do not just
> give them away to the first boy who smiles at you. But I do like the open
> communication between parent and child that is part of American culture. I think
> that by talking to your kids, which you see ads for that all the time. In the subway,
> talk to your kids about drugs and alcohol. You should also talk to your kids about
> sex! Why there are rules, what to look out for. Take the time and explain to them
> what honor is and how to keep it. We didn't have that with my parents growing
> up. I want that with my daughter.

Participant 9 discussed the importance of communication between parent and

child. She also discussed how the lack of that communication changed how she will

approach parenting her child. The values will stay the same in her parent child

relationship, but the delivery of the information will be more communicative, there will

be more dialogue regarding honor between her and her child.

> I had a hard adolescence due to my parents being strict and conservative. But the
> world is a much more dangerous place now than when I was growing up. Maybe
> that's why I thought my parents were being crazy, because it was nowhere near as
> bad as it is now. So, yea when I have kids, I will be strict but I want to make sure

they communicate with me. I didn't have that with my parents. I do now but not when I was young. And I think that would have helped a lot in our relationship. They never explained why. WHY do I have to stay home when all my friends get to go out? WHY is my virginity so important? It was just, you won't be able to get married. Now, I'll be able to tell my kids, look you shouldn't have sex because you can get pregnant, you can get sick. Sex is dangerous the way kids have it today. I would explain to my kids why it's better to wait, why it's better to have fewer partners. I don't know. Maybe I'll do a 180 when I actually have kids and pull my parents non-communicative, rule laden mentality. The world is pretty scary.

I want more open communication with me and my children than I had with my parents. I was scared to talk to my parents, to express my feelings about things like boys and sex. I think to really make sure my children understand how important honor is; I need them to be able to talk to me about things that would affect their choices to be honorable, especially girls. My experience of honor was one that was more controlled by my parents and their expectations. But with my children, I want them to have higher expectations for themselves. To value themselves. Not 100% because I want them to, but because THEY want to.

The first generation Levantine Arab American woman lives a life that is

conflicted. There is the desire to please her parents and the community from which she

comes, but there is also the desire to assimilate into Western/American culture. In living

in the more traditional way, she maintains her honor in the eyes of her family and her

community. This makes her a desirable prospect when young men her age are looking to

get married. Her education also adds to her ability to get married, however virginity is the

most valued characteristic of a prospective wife. The first generation Levantine Arab

American woman values honor and virginity, as it adds value to her personally and

socially. The concept of honor will still be valued in her future relationships with her

children. However, there is an emphasis on the value of communication between parent

and child that was lacking in her relationship with her parents. The first generation

Levantine Arab American woman plans to communicate to her child how important

honor is to her children and plans to explain why.

Summary

This chapter provided a discussion on the lived experience of honor among first generation Levantine Arab American women, using heuristic inquiry. The twelve co-researchers and the primary researcher herself contributed data, in the form of transcribed interviews and journal entries to illustrate the lived experience of honor. Direct quotes from the transcribed interviews and the journal entries were utilized to create a detailed description of the experience. Themes and patterns were identified as the primary researcher was immersed in the data and as they were discovered, they were supported with direct quotes. The primary researcher chose co-researchers whom she felt were the most exemplary in regards to the experience of honor being studied.

As each co-researcher described their experience of honor, five themes emerged. The theme of *Virginity* explained the understanding of virginity being located within the woman, how a woman is responsible for it, and how closely it must be guarded. *Social Status* was a theme that explained how one may be affected negatively socially by the loss of honor, how the family may suffer in regards to the choices of the individual. *Parental Role* was a theme in which the role of the parents was explained and explored by the primary and co-researchers. The parent's lack of communication and trust were central in this theme. The fourth theme of *Shame* involved the rules in place in the community, and how in breaking them, one can dishonor oneself and one's parents. By participating in inappropriate relationships and ignoring the importance of one's virginity. Lastly, the theme of *Looking Ahead.* The patterns that appeared within this theme were related to family respect, the trust between parent and child, the co-researcher's independence, and how the co-researcher's plan on developing relationships with their current or future children.

The next chapter summarizes and discusses the results of the data analysis further. The primary researcher will draw her conclusions about the study and discuss how it relates to the current literature. The primary researcher also discusses the limitations of the study and makes recommendations for future research. Finally, Chapter 5 presents the primary researcher's final thoughts on the research question, its findings, and any future implications.

CHAPTER 5. RESULTS, CONCLUSIONS, AND RECOMMENDATIONS

Introduction

The aim of Chapter 4 was to present the data for the study. The aim of Chapter 5 is to provide a summary of the study and a reflection on the findings. This study researched the lived experience of honor among first generation, Levantine, Arab American women. Following the discussion of the results, the primary researcher draws conclusions regarding the findings of the study and the relationship to the literature discussed in Chapter 2. In conclusion, the limitations of the study are discussed and the primary researcher provides recommendations for further research.

Summary of the Results

In a review of the current literature, it was found that there is a significant amount of research on Arab women, Islam, and honor killings (Abdo, 2006; Abu-Odeh, 2010; Bailey, 2009; Boosahda, 2003; Chesler, 2010; Faqir, 2001; Gilmore, 1987; Haddad, 1991, 2011; Hassan, 2000; Husseini, 2009; Madek, 2005; Peristiany & Pitt-Rivers, 1992; Peristiany, 1965; Stewart, 1994). However, there has not been a study that was used to explore how first generation, Levantine, Arab American women experience honor. Using Moustakas' (1990) heuristic method, the primary researcher was able to fill the gap in the literature. The study helps to illuminate the experience of honor among first generation, Arab American women specifically, how honor affects their everyday lives, relationships, and choices. The study sought to create an awareness of the importance of honor in the life of the first generation, Levantine, Arab American woman, in their community, and in relation to honor killings.

There has been an increase in the study of honor killings in the past 15 years due to the increase in the concentration of honor killings occurring in the United States (Jafri, 2008). The increasing rates of honor killings have been correlated to the increase in immigration of peoples from Arab and Muslim countries (Chesler, 2010; D'Agostino, 2002; Kayyali, 2005). These immigrants and their experience of acculturation has also been studied significantly by researchers (Berry, 2005; Daneshpour, 1998; Dwairy, 1997; Faragallah, Schumm, & Webb, 1997; Smith, 2011) There has also been a significant amount of research on honor killings, from why they are committed to how they are committed to by whom they are committed (Husseini, 2009; Nasrullah, Haqqi, & Cummings, 2009; Shaikh, Shaikh, Kamal, & Masood, 2010). As there is a significant amount of research regarding honor killings, the primary researcher did not focus on the act of honor killings during the data collection, as the experience of honor was the focus of the study.

The primary researcher is a first generation, Levantine, Arab American woman. Therefore a heuristic study was an appropriate researcher methodology to utilize for several reasons. First, the primary researcher was able to include her experience in the study. Secondly, the study was able to bring to light the experience of honor among first generation, Levantine, Arab American women using a qualitative approach that had not been used before regarding this specific experience. Finally, the topic of the experience of honor among first generation, Levantine, Arab American women is a topic that needs a more exploratory methodology to understand the experience at a deeper level.

Using Moustakas' (1990) heuristic methodology, 22 patterns with five main themes were identified by the primary researcher as they were related to the experience of honor among first generation, Levantine, Arab American women. These themes and patterns emerged from the data collected, which allowed the primary researcher to understand the experience of honor for the first generation, Levantine Arab American woman.

Patterns and Themes

The patterns are as follows:

- Forbidding Sex/Forbidding socializing with boys

- Education

- Honor resides in the Female body

- Importance of a "Good Marriage"

- Importance of Virginity

- Family rules

- Community rules

- Respect for your family

- Self-respect

- Inappropriate relationships

- Feelings of Shame

- Feelings of fear

- Guilt

- Modesty

- Being judged

- Being ostracized

- Trust between parent and child

- Disappointing your parent

- Independence

- Parents

- Lack of communication between parent and child

- Being a "Good girl"

The following six themes were identified by the primary researcher, as they allowed the researcher to illuminate the patterns further: Virginity, Social Status, Parental Role, Shame, and Relationships with children/future children.

The patterns were organized with the theme that the primary researcher felt best exemplified that theme:

- Theme 1: Virginity

    o Pattern 1.1: Honor resides in the Female body

    o Pattern 1.2: Self-respect

    o Pattern 1.3: Being a "good girl"

    o Pattern: 1.4: Modesty

- Theme 2: Social Status

    o Pattern 2.1: Being judged

    o Pattern 2.2 Being ostracized

    o Pattern 2.3: Education

    o Pattern 2.4: Importance of a "Good Marriage"

- Theme 3: Parental Role

  - o Pattern 3.1: Lack of Communication between parent and child

  - o Pattern 3.2: Forbidding Socializing with boys /Forbidding sex

  - o Pattern 3.3: Family Rules

  - o Pattern 3.4 Guilt

- Theme 4: Shame

  - o Pattern 4.1: Disappointing your parents

  - o Pattern 4.2: Inappropriate Relationships

  - o Pattern 4.3: Community Rules

  - o Pattern 4.4: Importance of virginity

- Theme 5: Looking Ahead

  - o Pattern 5.1 Trust between parent and child

  - o Pattern 5.2 Independence

  - o Pattern 5.3 Respect for your family

  - o Pattern 5.4 Relationships with Children/Future Children

After the primary researcher had identified the themes and patterns, three co-researchers were chosen that best illustrated the experience of honor. These exemplary portraits allowed the primary researcher to illustrate the themes and patterns discovered during the research process. All three co-researchers discussed the importance of honor in their everyday lives, the social impact of honor, and the relationship with current or future children.

Discussion of the Results

The research question that the study answered was "What is the lived experience of honor among first generation, Levantine, Arab American women?" Being a first generation, Levantine, Arab American woman, the primary researcher had the experience necessary to utilize the heuristic method to research the meaning of this experience. The primary researcher utilized the tools of Moustakas' (1990) heuristic methodology to gain not only a deeper understanding of her experience of honor but that of her co-researchers. As the primary researcher began to interview co-researchers and analyze the data collected, themes and patterns began to emerge. These themes and patterns were used to develop a vivid picture of the experience being studied, the experience of honor. The results of the study indicated to the primary researcher the importance of honor among first generation, Levantine, Arab American women.

The study revealed that the experience of honor among first generation Levantine Arab American women is complicated, both familial and societal, personal and public. It is an individual and collective experience. The experience begins at a young age and continues into motherhood. It is an ongoing and evolving experience, as the co-researcher aged and changed, so did her experience. Each co-researcher had an experience of honor that was similar to her other co-researchers and at the same time unique. Her memories and experiences were unique to her history, her family, and her upbringing.

In regards to limitations for this study, the primary researcher found that there were a few limitations. The first was a smaller sample size, as is prescribed by Moustakas' (1990) heuristic methodology. This may limit the generalization of the results but allowed for a more in-depth look at the phenomenon. A second limitation was the primary researcher's biases that could have affected the study. However, the researcher practiced self-awareness throughout the study, as was prescribed by Moustakas' (1990) heuristic methodology. The last limitation in the study was the lack of experience in heuristic research in the educational experience of the primary researcher. However, the primary researcher completed the following courses during her study at Capella University; Research Methods, Qualitative Analysis, Advanced Qualitative Analysis, and Quantitative Research Methods. In addition, the primary researcher did have experience working with qualitative data analysis and phenomenological studies. The study found that honor was experienced in several different ways; familial and social, personal and public, and individual and collective.

Familial and Societal

Each co-researcher discussed the role honor played in their lives but also, in the lives of their family members and how that affected them socially. It was emphasized that through their actions, they would either honor or dishonor themselves, which would directly affect their families socially, specifically, in regards to marriage and marriage prospects. "To be able to get married to a good man is the goal of most Arab mothers for their daughters, so if you do anything to dishonor yourself, you lose that chance at a good marriage." The dishonor bleeds into the rest of your family. The familial relationship hinges on the female child's behavior and whether or not it is honorable. If it is, then she shows the family and the world that she respects her parents and family. If she does not behave honorably, she is showing her parents and the world that she does not respect them. By breaking the rules set out for her by her family, it indicates to society that she does not respect her parents. The familial component of honor is evident in Patterns 6 (family rules), 8 (respect for your family), 17 (trust between parent and child, and 18 (disappointing your parent).

The co-researchers' narratives agreed in that the aftermath of one's actions could have a damaging effect on the family members, "Your shame is contagious to your family though. It affects them socially. People won't talk to them, their kids won't hang out with your kids, and when you get older you aren't an acceptable option for marriage." The co-researchers agreed that society had an equal role in the pressure put on these young women to behave a certain way. As they were growing up the primary pressure was from their parents. However, as they matured, it became clear to them that the only reason there was pressure from their parents was due to their parents feeling pressure from society. If there were no standards set to achieve by society, if the label of "good girl" was not in place, perhaps there would not be pressure on behalf of the parent to ensure their daughters live an honorable life. This social component of honor is evident in Patterns 4 (importance of a good marriage), 7 (community rules), 15 (being judged), and 16 (being ostracized). This societal stigma is not easily removed. Once the honor of a young girl has been lost, her family is affected by it continually. Social niceties stop, invitations cease to arrive, and they are isolated completely.

Personal and Public

Virginity is a topic that is, in most cultures and countries, off limits and private. However, in Arab and Muslim culture and countries, the topic is widely discussed. Perhaps not in the wide open, but the conversation as to who is or is not a virgin is one that is often had. The importance placed on virginity, a private thing for a young girl very quickly becomes public when it comes time for marriage.

It is something that is personal, sure, but it's also something that is discussed. Who is and who isn't. I don't think that it's normal conversation in other homes. Probably not in the way it is in our homes.

It was always something that I did not want anyone knowing. I mean even on my wedding night, I knew people assumed I wasn't a virgin anymore but I felt like it was something that was so private and mine and now it was no longer mine. Because everyone knew, my husband's family wanted to be sure.

The co-researchers agreed that virginity was the number one indicator of honor. Without it, you were not valued, wanted, or respected. Patterns 3 (honor resides in the body), 4 (importance of marriage), 11 (feelings of shame), 12 (feelings of guilt), and 22 (being a good girl) indicate where virginity had a dominant place in the lives of the co-researchers.

The public image of a "good girl" was a pattern that repeated in all the co-researchers' narratives. "I was the oldest, the good daughter. I needed to maintain my family's honor. It was the most important thing I did." This sentiment was reflected over and over again in the narrative of the co-researchers; "I couldn't just do what I wanted, I had to be the good girl. To make my parents proud, I had to stay a virgin til I was married." Being labeled as such had largely due to with virginity, but also had to do with the co-researcher's behavior in general. The Patterns 2 (education), 8 (respect for your family), 14 (modesty), 18 (disappointing your parent), and 22 (being a "good girl), were collectively part of a public image that each co-researcher looked to maintain. It seemed that if their exterior persona were put together, it was less likely the important component of the image, virginity, would be questioned. However, virginity would be, largely, the deciding and sometimes damning factor.

Individual and Collective

In the Arab or Muslim household, the needs and wants of the individual come secondary to the needs of the family as a whole. What is better for the greater good is usually what is pursued. This does not leave much room for the individual to make choices based solely on their own wants. In the case of the first generation Levantine Arab American women, the co-researchers were born here and may have more individualistic personalities that come into conflict with the more collective personalities of their parents, who were born and raised abroad.

> I had to make a hard choice, what I wanted versus what my parents wanted. It was not easy, and there is still a rift between us, but I made the best choice for me. I don't think I should have to live to make anyone but me happy.

This conflict between individual and collective good was not a new concept for the primary researcher; it was one she had been dealing with her entire life. Sometimes the conflict was internal, where she would weigh out her decisions based on her wants. Sometimes the conflict was external, with her parent and what was thought to be best for the family, for the long term. Patterns 6 (family rules), 8 (respect for family), 9 (self-respect), 19 (independence), 20 (parents) and 21 (lack of communication between parent and child) are illustrative in the constant conflict between the traditional parent and the assimilated child. There is a difference not only of opinion but also on what is valuable to each side. Co-researchers are in agreement that a way to remedy this situation is communication. In fact, it is a trait in relationships they hope to have well established with their own children someday.

The lived experience of honor among first generation, Levantine Arab American women is one that is continuously changing as she changes. She changes from little girl, to pubescent woman, to married woman, and to mother. At each stage in her life, honor is central. In addition, at each stage, the co-researchers described the struggle to maintain honor. The co-researcher described the burden of their honor. And for some, it was a burden worth carrying.

Discussion of the Conclusions

This study contributed to the existing literature and the field of psychology by illuminating the experience of honor for the first generation, Levantine, Arab American woman. The primary researcher chose the heuristic approach due to her intense interest and shared experience with the phenomenon being studied. As such, there were no hypotheses set in place to be proven or disproved by the primary researcher to answer the research question: What is the lived experience of honor of first generation, Levantine, Arab American women? The results of the heuristic study supported the primary researcher's inclination that first generation, Levantine, Arab American women have an intense experience of honor in their lives, whether it was positive or negative. The primary researcher identified that there was a gap in the literature regarding the experience of honor within this specific community. The primary researcher took care to highlight where the literature was substantial and supportive of the research question. The literature is considerable in the areas of immigration, assimilation, and acculturation (D'Agostino, 2002; Duderija, 2008; Sam & Berry, 2010), Islam (Hamid, 2008; Zentella, 2010), Women and Islam (Ahmed, 1992; Barlas, 2002; Beck and Keddie, 1980; Sabbah, 1984; Wadud, 1999), honor (Peristiany & Pitt-Rivers, 1992; Peristiany, 1965; Stewart, 1994); , and honor killings (Husseini, 2009).

As discussed by Duderija (2008), the co-researchers did experience a crisis of identity as first generation, Levantine Arab American women. The co-researchers expressed a strong desire to fit in, to "act American" and leave behind their parent's traditions. Stressors due to assimilation and acculturation have been explored fully in the aforementioned research and proved true when exploring the experiences of the co-researchers. Co-researchers expressed feelings of anger, resentment, and frustration regarding their family's traditions and their new culture in the United States. Since 9/11 and the numerous terror attacks since then, there is no shortage of literature on Islam and women and Islam in general. In regards to Islam, the literature conducted since the 9/11 attacks have been informative in regards to what Muslims believe. Islam, while one of the fastest growing religions in the world, had not been a faith in which most Americans were familiar. After the attacks, there were many books and articles asking and answering the question of "What do Muslims believe?" In Hamid's (2008) article, *Basic history and tenets of Islam: A brief introduction,* the reader is given an in-depth introduction to the Islamic faith. From Muhammed and his tribal background, his family history, and the revelations from God to Islamic law (Sharia) and faith practices. In regards to women and Islam, there had been much research, but the most prominent was the work of Leila Ahmed. In her book *Women and Gender in Islam: Historical Roots of a Modern Debate,* Ahmed (1992) reviewed the role of women spanning from pre-Islamic times, through Islamic history, to the early 21st century. Her work was foundational and is often referenced by anyone writing about women and Islam.

In regards to the literature on honor (Peristiany & Pitt-Rivers, 1992; Peristiany, 1965; Stewart, 1994) and honor killings (Husseini, 2009), the co-researchers expressed sentiments in agreement with the point made in both areas of research. The point made on research by Peristiany (1965) and Peristiany and Pitt-Rivers (1992) is that there is an emphasis on the behaviors of men and women, but particularly women. These behaviors are more focused on the sexual purity and honor of the individual and how that can affect the morality of the larger community, or the family. Stewart's (1994) definition of honor is twofold: objectified and subjectified. The co-researchers experience reflected that there were two types of honor, one that you give yourself and one that society gives you. Honor is central in both, however, the distributor changes. Co-researcher's did not speak upon honor killings much. It appeared that though they were aware of such acts of violence, one co-researcher making it clear that her parents would never do such a thing, it was not something they were concerned with or worried about in their experience of honor. The primary researcher hypothesized that the phenomenon of honor killings would not be discussed during the interviews because the co-researchers did not have any experience, personally, with honor killings. However, their experience of honor, as a phenomenon, was very rich.

In regards to honor killings, there has been extensive research by journalists. The journalist who has focused on the phenomenon of honor killings is Rana Husseini (2009). In her book, *Murder in the Name of Honor* (Husseini, 2009), Husseini interviews several women who have been attacked by male family members. The women have had attempts on their lives for the family to regain honor lost based on their actions. Husseini (2009) profiles the woman's experience in the event of honor killing. To gain access to the male perspective in honor killings, the work of Ayse Onal (2008) is critical. In her book, *Honour Killing: Stories of men who killed,* she conducted interviews of men who have been convicted and are serving sentences for killing or attempting to kill their female family members. These women are their sisters, their mothers, their cousins, their daughters. These two works are foundational in regards to the phenomenon. They give researchers a male and female perspective in regards to the phenomenon.

However, for a more structured understanding of a foundation in research, the studies conducted by Recep Doğan (2014a, 2014b, 2016) give this structured foundation in honor killings. Doğan conducted a three-part study. The first was a research study to understand the concept of culture that inspires honor killing (Doğan, 2014a). Following this study, Doğan (2014b) delved into profiling the victims and the aggressors in honor killing cases, specifically in Turkey, "The dynamics of honor killings and the perpetrator's experiences." Finally, Doğan (2016) focused on seeking out "qualified information about the patterns, dynamics, and the chain of events that culminate in murder in such femicide cases" (p. 54). Doğan uses the perpetrator's voice and story to create a descriptive picture of the killings and the motivations behind them. These three studies are informative and incredibly descriptive regarding the experience of honor killings. However, they are limited in that they are focused on Turkey and Turkish culture. While there are some shared experiences, there needs to be a set of studies like this in all Middle Eastern countries. As was previously theorized, honor can be different geographically. There have been studies that focus on honor killings in countries like Jordan (Husseini, 2009), Turkey (Doğan, 2011, 2014b, 2016), and Pakistan (Shaikh, Kamal, & Naqvi, 2015). However, there is still a need for studies regarding the experience of honor across the Middle East.

A few limitations have been previously discussed and should be expanded upon here. The first was the age restrictions on the potential participants. There were several who expressed a desire to participate in the study. However, they were under 18 and not in the age range of the study's criteria for participation. The second was the small sample size of 13 co-researchers. The study being heuristic called for a smaller sample size. However, it limits the experiences studied and analyzed. Therefore, the experience explored in this study cannot be applied to all first generation, Levantine, Arab American women. The third limitation is that on behalf of the primary researcher. This was the first time she had utilized the heuristic method as it was outlined by Moustakas (1990). However, she did have experience utilizing qualitative data analysis. A fourth limitation was due to the sample being confined to a smaller area of the world. As was previously mentioned, honor is experienced differently all across the world. It can differ from country to country. Therefore, by focusing on honor as it is experienced in the United States limited the study. Even further, the study being conducted in the states of New York, New Jersey, Connecticut, Massachusetts, California, Nevada, Wyoming, and Florida limited the study.

Recommendations for Future Research or Interventions

This research study has opened a few areas for future study. One area would be a study on women who have survived attempts at their life in an honor killing. There are several cases of attempted honor killing in the United States (Ackerman & Block, 1999; Spencer, 2008; Stelloh & Barron, 2011; Tarabay, 2009). The survivors would be able to give detailed insight in regards to the experience, the motivations behind the attempts on their lives, and the relationships with the family members that are ordered to end their lives. A case study organized by religion and or country of origin would be informative regarding this crisis.

Another area for further study would involve a study on the men who are pushed to regain their family's honor by killing their dishonored female family members. Husseini (2009) interviewed a number of men incarcerated for attempted murder to regain the family honor lost due to the dishonorable actions of a female family member. While the interviews inform the reader regarding motivation, murder weapons, and prison sentences, there needs to be a deeper understanding of the experience of the male when he is asked to murder in the name of his family's honor. A qualitative study, specifically a phenomenological one would be insightful from this experience.

An area for future study would require larger sample sizes to determine whether the themes and patterns discovered in this study would be applicable to the larger population. A suggestion to conduct a phenomenological study or several case studies in each geographical region of the United States (Northeast, Southwest, Northwest, and Southwest) may be a manageable way to gather more information with a larger group of participants. In addition, perhaps separating participants by country would be helpful in the study of the experience of honor among first generation, Levantine, Arab American women. Women, who are Egyptian American, Jordanian American, Syrian American, etc., may have different experiences of honor, simply based on their parents' country of origin. A better understanding of honor based on country of origin and by region in the United States would further contribute to the existing literature. Perhaps a future study could be conducted to include the age group of 15-24.

A quantitative study that would add to the existing literature on honor would be a quantitative study looking into surveying the number of young women who may feel they are at risk for honor killing. Perhaps a survey as to whether or not it is an acceptable form of punishment for acting out of societal and familial norms. Another quantitative study that would be helpful is one that would measure the correlation between religion and the incidence of honor killing. Does the level of religiousness correlate to the occurrence of honor killing?

Another area of future research would be a phenomenological study exploring the experience of women who have had attempts on their lives in the name of honor. What is the experience had by that group of women? A study in that area would provide a deeper understanding of not only the experience of honor killing but also the familial relationships in families that value honor to the point of killing to regain it.

Conclusion

Previous studies have explored the concept of honor, the phenomenon of honor killings, the role of Islam in the lives of Arab women, and Arab culture. However, no study has focused on the lived experience of honor among first generation, Levantine, Arab American women. The experiences of these women are complex and connected to various parts of their lives: the social, the familial, the personal, and the public. These co-researchers have demonstrated, through their shared experiences, that there is a constant struggle between the self and society. There a complexity in deciding what is for the good of the group as opposed to the desires of the individual.

Co-researchers have agreed in their statements regarding their choices not really being their own. The long-term effects always had to be weighed and considered, actions that were and were not worth social exclusion. One always had to think ahead and think inclusively of her family. How would this choice affect my marriage choices? Would it affect my parents? Would it negatively influence my siblings and their prospects? The experience of honor in this study included its separating and cohesive nature in the lives of first generation, Levantine, Arab American women.

There are many implications of this first study regarding the experience of honor among first generation, Levantine, Arab American women. The results of the study indicate that honor is central to one's personal value, social value, the value of their family, marriageability, social inclusion, and familial harmony. The findings indicate that even though the co-researchers lived in the United States, their lives were still very much covered by the traditions that were practiced in their parent's home countries. Furthermore, the actions that they take on a daily basis could affect their long-term marriage choices, their female family member's long-term marriage choices, and their parent's ability to be accepted and welcomed by their own communities. Honor is a communal value in the Arab American community. Females are the guardians and the gatekeepers of the honor of the family and eventually the honor of their communities. Once lost, it is difficult to regain if at all possible.